NO LONGER PROPERTY OF
SEATTLE PUBLIC LIBRARY

PHYSICS FOR
MEN

D1040674

PHYSICS FOR MEN

THE SCIENCE BEHIND BEING A GUY

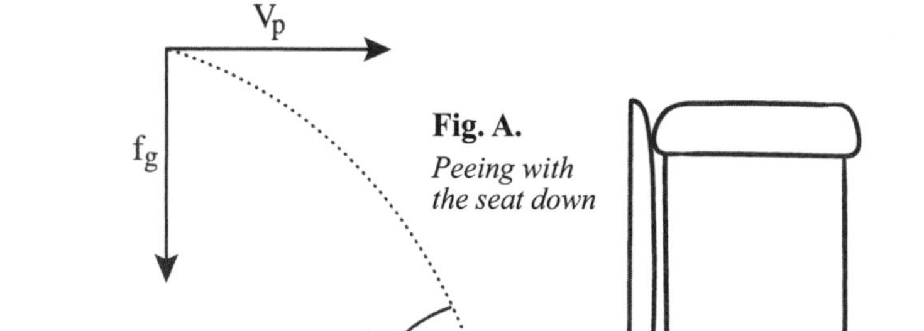

V_p
f_g
θ
d

Fig. A.
Peeing with the seat down

P. R. KELT

adamsmedia
AVON, MASSACHUSETTS

Copyright © 2012 by F+W Media, Inc.
All rights reserved.
This book, or parts thereof, may not be reproduced in any
form without permission from the publisher; exceptions are
made for brief excerpts used in published reviews.

Published by
Adams Media, a division of F+W Media, Inc.
57 Littlefield Street, Avon, MA 02322. U.S.A.
www.adamsmedia.com

ISBN 10: 1-4405-1279-5
ISBN 13: 978-1-4405-1279-7
eISBN 10: 1-4405-2693-1
eISBN 13: 978-1-4405-2693-0

Printed in the United States of America.

10   9   8   7   6   5   4   3   2

Library of Congress Cataloging-in-Publication Data
is available from the publisher.

This publication is designed to provide accurate and authoritative information with regard
to the subject matter covered. It is sold with the understanding that the publisher is not
engaged in rendering legal, accounting, or other professional advice. If legal advice or
other expert assistance is required, the services of a competent professional person should
be sought.
—From a *Declaration of Principles* jointly adopted by a Committee of the American Bar
Association and a Committee of Publishers and Associations

Certain sections of the book deal with activities that may result in serious bodily harm
or even death. The authors, Adams Media, and F+W Media, Inc. do not accept liability
for any injury, loss, legal consequence, or incidental or consequential damage incurred by
reliance on the information or advice provided in this book. The information in this book
is for entertainment purposes only.

Illustrations by Eric Andrews.

This book is available at quantity discounts for bulk purchases.
For information, please call 1-800-289-0963.

CONTENTS

INTRODUCTION

Sports are fun. *Physics is not.*

Partying is fun. *Physics is not.*

Women are fun. *Physics is not.*

Understood—physics is not fun. But what if you could use physics to *have* fun? What if all the equations and variables, formulas and principles lead to better odds on the basketball court, better times at the bar, and better luck with the ladies? Then physics is definitely fun.

In this physics re-education, the focus is on what physics can do for you. Forget Ohm and Einstein. This is your time to shine—and get what you want. Things are no longer left up to chance. It's time to reveal the math and science to perfect your every action (or inaction). Whether it's acing a serve or serving up a drink like Cruise in *Cocktail*, the fundamentals are broken down step-by-step and put into terms you'll understand. It's not rocket science. It's guy physics.

And while we're emphasizing the fun stuff, the science is grounded in reality. You're still going to use the same concepts and principles tackled in high school. Angles will be calculated, velocities figured, and equations ran. Except this time around, the outcome is more interesting than some metal runner propelling down a track. Instead, it's figuring out the correct trajectory a piece of popcorn needs to travel in order to land in your mouth, or the proper release angle for a successful shot during quarters. It's just as involved, just not as boring.

It starts with the applications of guy physics as it pertains to eating and drinking, so you're all set whether you're lighting up the grill or putting back a pint. Then chapters on entertainment and sports will show you how to take command of any arena from the Beirut table to the pool table. There's even a chapter dedicated to doing things around the house—or more accurately, *not* doing things around the house as it helps you get out of your chores. The section on women reveals picking up ladies is a science, not an art. And while sleeping might seem intuitive, there's a difference between doing something and doing something *well*. It's all topped off with a collection of feats that any man would consider great—from diving off hundred-foot-high cliffs to dealing with mothers-in-law.

Consider this your new textbook for success. The topics covered will give you a well-rounded education in what it means to be a man. And it will teach you that physics can be fun.

LESSONS IN THIS CHAPTER

EATING AND DRINKING

1.a STEAL FOOD FROM YOUR FRIEND'S PLATE

While watching the game, food is a necessity. The more the better. A great way to get more is by poaching the food your bud already has on his plate (that way, you don't even have to get up off the couch). Obviously, the most delicious foods are the most desirable—and the most protected. Luckily, you have not only the art of surprise in your favor, but also the distraction of the game and the other dudes hanging out. The protection quotient, P_q, tells you how fast and sneaky you need to be. It is calculated as:

$$P_q = \frac{Y_{um} - S_v}{\sqrt[3]{V_F} + 1}$$

where Y_{um} is the desirability coefficient, S_v is the variable for the look of hunger satiation on your bud's face (on a scale of 1 to 10), and V_F is the amount of the desired food by volume on the plate. The desirability coefficient for select foods can be read off the Good Game Day Food Chart determined by T. D. Williams using double-blind, mouth-wide-open taste testing.

FOOD	DESIRABILITY COEFFICIENT
Chalk	−0.3
Celery stick, no peanut butter	0.7
Chicken wings, barbeque	9.9

Figure 1.1. Good Game Day Food Chart by T. D. Williams

Another important factor to consider is the distraction factor, D. The distraction factor depends on a few items: emotional involvement in the game, E_m, as well as the emotional involvement of those in your vicinity. If you can manage the latter, you'll have no need to calculate further as D will be so large that it will swamp all other considerations. You can go ahead and plunder at will.

Otherwise, calculate *D* as:

$$D = \sum_I \frac{\cot(\theta_I)}{d_I} + E_m$$

The summation is over the number of friends in the room other than you and your victim.

Emotional involvement, E_m, falls on a scale of 1 to 10. For representative values,

$$\begin{aligned} d_1 &= 0.70m \\ \theta_1 &= 70^\circ \\ d_2 &= 1.1m \\ \theta_2 &= 80^\circ \\ E_m &= 5.6 \\ Y_{um} &= 9.9 \\ S_V &= 2 \\ V_F &= 0.02m^3 \end{aligned}$$

We get:

$$P_q = \frac{9.9 - 2}{\sqrt[3]{0.02} + 1} = 6.21$$

$$D = \frac{\cot(70^\circ)}{0.7} + \frac{\cot(80^\circ)}{1.1} + 5.6 = 6.28$$

Since $D > P_q$, you should make an attempt at the item of desire.

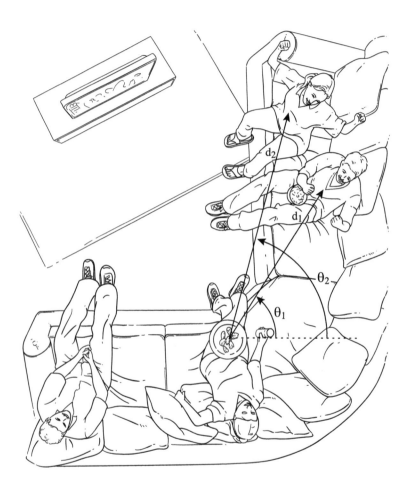

Fig. 1.a Steal Food from Your Friend's Plate.

1.b CARVE A TURKEY

Carving a turkey in the presence of friends and family takes a sure hand and nerves of steel. Slice it too thick, and you lose cred. The thinner it is, the better. However, those desirably thin slices will fall to pieces like an outdoor deck put together with thumbtacks, so the utmost care must be exercised. What will you do? Use Newton's Second Law to make you look like a Turkey Day Champ. While you are slicing, the slice is going to be subjected to a force (F) equal to the slice's mass (m) times its acceleration (a). You will manage the force so you don't destroy your righteously thin slice, while at the same time garnering style points. The style points come from allowing the slice to fall away gracefully from the turkey breast (the ladies love this).

First, balance out the force:

$$Fd_M \sin\theta_M = mgd_S \sin\theta_S$$

$$d_m = L - d$$

$$d_s = \frac{L - l}{2}$$

Now, solve for F, the force you will apply:

$$F = \frac{mgd_S \sin\theta_S}{d_M \sin\theta_M}$$

The S_{tyle} value depends on the angles and distances involved:

$$S_{tyle} = \frac{a_1 d_M \theta_M^2}{m} - a_2 C^3$$

The C in this equation is the number of breaks in the slice; a_1 and a_2 are multiplicative constants with the values:

$$a_1 = 1 \times style \times kg/1m \times \deg$$

$$a_2 = 1,000 \times style/breaks^3$$

Large S_{tyle} values are the best. Here are some calculations to give you a goal for which to shoot—this model will be a slice of deli size and thickness:

$$m = 0.1kg$$
$$d_m = 0.012m$$
$$\theta_M = 28.87°$$

For these values, you will achieve 100 style points. Of course, this is for $C = 0$, because you are good like that! Go for it and impress the guests!

θ_M
d
l
L
mg
θ_S

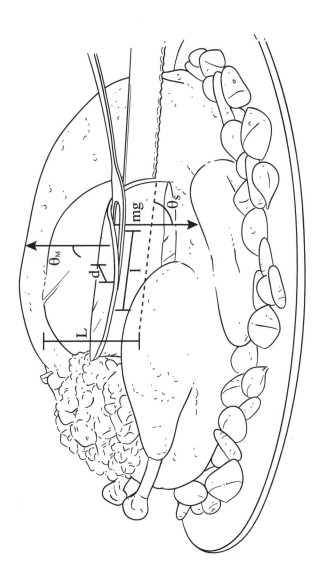

Fig. 1.b Carve a Turkey

1.c FILLET A FISH

Now that you are a Turkey Day Champ, it's time to set your sights on the turkeys of the sea. Think of it as an advanced application of turkey carving. The plan is to make a "bow tie" for your fillet out of fish guts. The key here is maintaining the correct amount of friction between your fingers and the guts. The important physics involved in this deals with the coefficient of friction between guts and fingers. We'll call it μ. Here's the equation for the force of friction:

$$F = \mu N$$

So the bigger μ is, the greater the force of friction. For slimy guts, it will be small. N in the equation stands for what's called the normal force. It is the force with which you can pinch your fingers together. You will overcome the small coefficient of friction with brute force! Be careful though: The failure strength of fish guts isn't very high. You avoid exceeding this with your manly brute force. Apply Newton's Laws again for balancing forces:

$$2\mu N = T_{guts}$$

Typical values might be:

$$\mu = 0.02$$
$$T_{guts} = 0.01 N$$

With these values, your max pinching force is:

$$N = \frac{T_{guts}}{2\mu} = \frac{0.01 newton}{0.02} = \frac{1}{4} newton$$

This is the force it takes to lift 1/20 of a pound. The advanced and revised style points become:

$$S_{tyle} = \frac{a_1 d_M \theta_M^2}{m} - a_2 C^3 + A_{Bow}$$

The last term is the area of the bow you tie. The bigger, the better!

N
Tguts

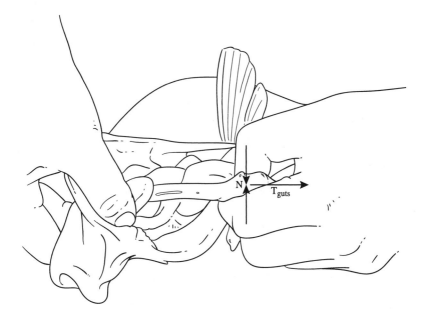

Fig. 1.c Fillet a Fish

1.d FIRE UP THE GRILL

Explosions are cool. Getting the grill going is just an excuse for creating a minor conflagration.

You need the charcoal, lighter fluid, and a match. Simple. To maximize the boom factor, *BF*, you

want to maximize the volume of lighter fluid relative to the volume of the charcoal. Too much is

too much boom factor; not enough is just lame. You will experimentally determine how much is

enough by pouring the fluid into a graduated beaker. Take note of the volume in the beaker, V_s.

Now add one briquette to the beaker, let it soak for at least half an hour, and then remove.

Record the final volume in the beaker, V_f. Now calculate the max *BF* for a half-hour soak:

$$BF = \left(\frac{V_s - V_f}{V_s} \right)^{-1}$$

Take advantage of this by counting out the number of briquettes you place in the grill. The

correct volume of lighter fluid for this number *N* is now:

$$V_{BOOM} = \frac{V_s}{BF} \times N$$

You are set to burn. To ignite, calculate the correct vertical angle (θ) and velocity (*vy*) at which

to throw a match into the grill from a safe distance of 10 feet. You will need the equations of

projectile motion. You will forego the possibility of the match going out in flight by launching it

while the phosphorus in the match head is still in the process of igniting. This takes about 2

seconds. Let:

$$t = 2s$$
$$d = 10\,ft$$
$$h_o = 4\,ft$$
$$h_g = 3\,ft$$

A 2-second time of flight gives a horizontal velocity of:

$$v_x = \frac{d}{t} = \frac{10\,ft}{2s} = 5\,ft/s$$

The initial vertical velocity is:

$$v_y = \frac{h_g - h_o + \frac{1}{2}at^2}{t} = \frac{63\,ft}{2s} = 31.5\,ft/s$$

Now you can find the launch angle:

$$\theta = \tan^{-1}\frac{v_y}{v_x} = \tan^{-1}\frac{31.5\,ft/s}{5\,ft/s} = 80.98°$$

That is a sweet launch with nice arc! Job well done! Now run for the pool to put out that pesky

fire that started on your head (see Sports: Soak Sunbathers with a Monster Cannonball).

V
V_x
V_y
θ
h_m
h_g
h_o
d

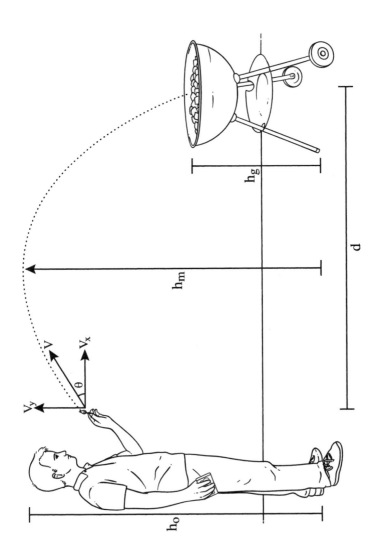

Fig. 1.d Fire Up the Grill

1.e ORDER AND CONSUME PIZZA WITHOUT LEAVING THE LA-Z-BOY

You will use both your Man Physics and your natural, wily skills to accomplish this with appropriate efficiency and timing. First, dial the phone using as little energy as possible. Compare the energy required to lift and move a finger to push a number on the phone with that necessary to slide a finger the same distance on the keypad.

The amount of energy—or work (W)—expended equals the force (F) of the task multiplied by the distance (d) over which it occurs:

$$W = Fd$$

The equation for work expended while lifting and moving is slightly more complicated, as it also takes into account the mass of the object (m), the force of gravity (g), and the height to which the object is lifted (h):

$$W_l = mgh + F_{move}d_d$$

F_{move} is about 1/6 of a newton•ml for muscle.

The muscle moving the finger is about 1 ml, so F_{move} = 1/6 N.

Now calculate the work it would take to overcome the friction of your finger moving against the keypad (W_d):

$$W_d = mg\mu d_d$$

In this case, the coefficient of kinetic friction, μ, will be about 0.6. Say that for lifting, you would lift about 1 centimeter.

To compare the work of lifting your finger to the work of dragging it, set up this equation to find the exertion constant:

$$m = 0.04\,kg$$
$$g = 9.8\,m/s^2$$
$$h = 0.01\,m$$
$$F_{move} = 0.17N$$
$$d_d = 0.02\,m$$
$$\mu = 0.6$$

$$Exertion = \frac{W_l}{W_d} = \frac{mgh + F_{move}d_d}{mg\mu d_d} = \frac{0.007}{0.004} = 1.8$$

An exertion value greater than 1 means that you should drag and not lift. After dialing, you have

enough energy to ask your significant other to cuddle on your lap while the pizza is on the way.

This isn't just a ploy for brownie points. You also do it because you know that when the pizza

comes, she will have to get up first. And of course, since you have enraptured her with your

kisses, she will run to the door, pay for the pizza, and be back in your lap with it before you can

drag your finger across the keypad of the remote control.

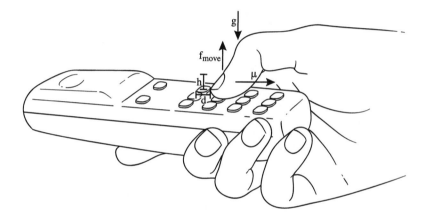

Fig. 1.e Order and Consume Pizza Without Leaving the La-Z-Boy

1.f SINK A NAPKIN IN THE GARBAGE

Whether you play basketball or not, sinking a balled-up napkin into the trash can just feel good. It feels even better when people are watching. The likelihood that you are going to make the shot depends on your audience, the shot distance, and your confidence. Use the shot factor to figure out how likely you are to make it:

$$ShotFactor = \frac{N_T(N_W + 1)}{(D - 1.8m)^{3/2}}C$$

$N_T = TotalAudience$
$N_W = Numberofwomen$
$D = ShotLength$
$C = Confident(Scaleof1 - 10inunitsofm^{3/2}/number)$

In this example, you are hanging around after the holiday office party with 4 people, 2 of whom are women, there's a garbage can about 2 meters away, and you just downed a few whiskey sours so you are feeling pretty confident (7.3). With these variables, your ShotFactor is:

$$ShotFactor = \frac{4 \times (2 + 1)}{(2m - 1.8m)^{3/2}} \times 7.3m^{3/2}/number = 979$$

That's pretty high, so begin calculating your trajectory parameters. You want to impress the audience, and the ladies especially, so you opt for a longer hang time of 1.5 seconds. With your confidence level, make it a jump shot. Your initial height is then 1.9 meters. The garbage can is 1.0 meter high. So:

$$v_y = \frac{1.0m - 1.9m + \frac{1}{2}9.8\frac{m}{s^2}(1.5s)^2}{1.5s} = \frac{10.13m}{1.5s} = 6.75m/s$$

$$v_x = \frac{2m}{1.5} = 1.33m/s$$

You next calculate the release angle for the shot:

$$\theta = \tan^{-1}\frac{6.75m/s}{1.33m/s} = 78.85^{o}$$

You make the shot, much to the delight of the audience, though not particularly surprising to you, since you used your Man Physics to get the job done.

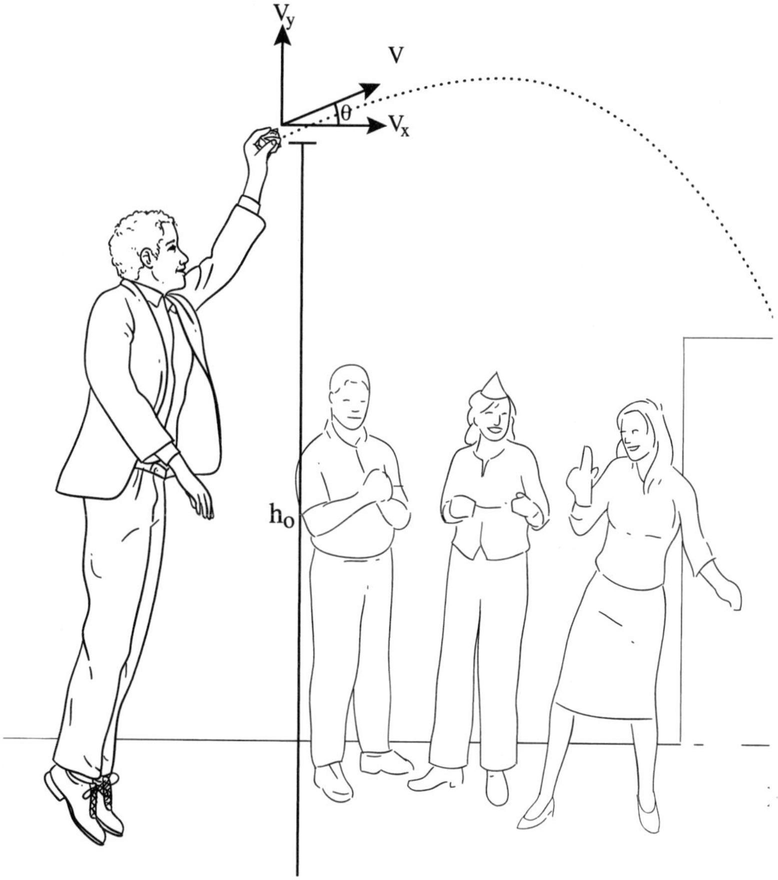
Vy
V
θ
Vx
ho

Fig. 1.f Sink a Napkin in the Garbage

1.g CATCH POPCORN IN YOUR MOUTH

An advanced application of projectile motion is catching popcorn in your mouth. You know that the key is launching the popcorn high enough to react to the popcorn mid-flight. So you opt for a maximum height of the popcorn of 0.8 meter. You throw from a distance of 0.5 meter from hand to mouth. Calculate the time of flight:

$$v_x = \frac{d}{t} = \frac{0.5m}{0.32s} = 1.56\frac{m}{s}$$

Find the horizontal and vertical speed and the release angle:

$$v_x = \frac{d}{t} = \frac{0.5m}{0.32s} = 1.56\frac{m}{s}$$

$$v_y = gt = 9.8\frac{m}{s} \times 0.32s = 3.14\frac{m}{s}$$

$$\theta = \tan^{-1}\frac{3.14m/s}{1.56m/s} = 63.6^{\circ}$$

Now throw. But wait! Something is amiss! You realize that upon your throw, you leaned back in your chair and it started toppling over backwards. The horizontal speed with which you were moving in your chair when you launched was added to your initial horizontal throw speed. Quickly recalculate the distance the popcorn will now travel and where your mouth must be to catch it:

$$v_{x_{new}} = v_x + v_{x_{fall}} = 1.56\frac{m}{s} + 0.11\frac{m}{s} = 1.67\frac{m}{s}$$

$$d_{new} = v_{x_{new}}t = 1.67\frac{m}{s} \times 0.32s = 0.534$$

Extend the additional 0.034 meter and catch the popcorn. Of course you come crashing down on the floor after the catch, but you had to take one for the team (of one). Now the admiration of your female coworkers is mixed with concern for your health, and as you munch on the spectacularly acquired popcorn, you can bask in their concerns and caresses.

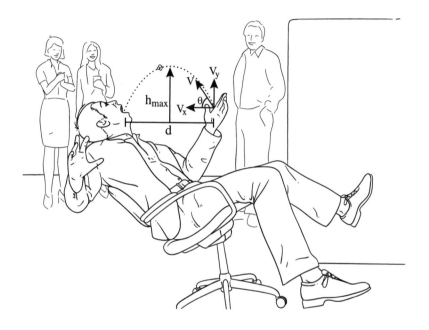

Fig. 1.g Catch Popcorn in Your Mouth

1.h DRINK FROM THE MILK CONTAINER WITHOUT SPILLING ANY MILK

Drinking straight out of the carton is too satisfying not to do it. The question is: How fast can you drink it without spilling? First, figure out how fast you can swallow. The volume of your swallow is 70 milliliters, and it takes you 0.4 second to swallow. So drinking speed while standing is:

$$S_{drink} = \frac{0.07l}{0.4s} = 0.18\frac{l}{s}$$

Now, figure the approximate speed at which milk leaves the carton for a certain height of the fluid (h_f) at the triangular part of the opening:

$$S_{milk} = A_o\sqrt{2g\frac{h_f}{3}}$$
$$A_o = A\cos\theta$$
$$h_f = h\cos\theta$$

For an A of 0.0006 square meter and h of 0.02 meter, you find the angle at which you can hold the carton to reach S_{drink}:

$$S_{milk} = S_{drink}$$
$$A\cos\theta\sqrt{gh\cos\theta} = 0.18\frac{l}{s} \times \frac{m^3}{1000l} = 0.00018\frac{m^3}{s}$$

$$\cos\theta = \sqrt[3]{\frac{\left(\dfrac{0.00018\dfrac{m^3}{s}}{0.0006m^2}\right)^2}{\dfrac{2}{3}\times 9.8m/s^2 \times 0.02m}}$$

$$\theta = \cos^{-1}\left(\sqrt[3]{\frac{\left(\dfrac{0.00018\dfrac{m^3}{s}}{0.0002m^2}\right)^2}{9.8m^2/s^2 \times 0.02m}}\right) = 46.5°$$

Note: No matter how successful you become at this precisely calculated maneuver, it is probably

best not to perform it in the presence of a woman who does not already find you irresistible.

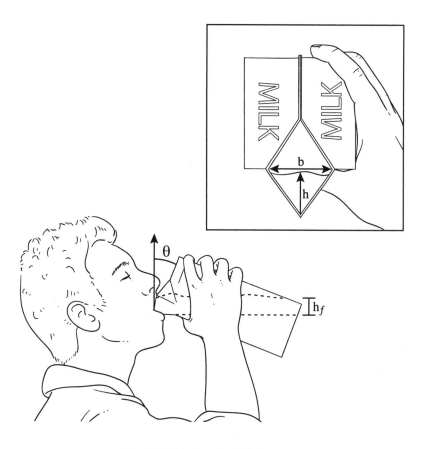

Fig. 1.h Drink from the Milk Container
Without Spilling Any Milk

1.i DOWN A PINT IN ONE SWIG

With the milk under your belt, up the ante by downing a pint. The added difficulty you must consider is the effect of carbonation on the speed of your swallow. Essentially, the fizz of CO_2 will decrease your normal swallowing speed (S_{drink}) by an amount known as the foaming factor (*FF*). First calculate the amount of gas released in a pour of beer by the size of the head:

$$\mathrm{V_{foam}} = \frac{\pi \mathrm{h}}{3}\left(\mathrm{R}^2 + \mathrm{Rr} + \mathrm{r}^2\right)$$
$$= \frac{\pi \times 0.015\mathrm{m}}{3}\left(0.0012\mathrm{m}^2 + 0.007\mathrm{m}^2 + 0.0004\mathrm{m}^2\right) = 0.000037\mathrm{m}^2$$

From this, the fizz factor is:

$$FF = 1 - \frac{V_{foam}}{V_{beer} + V_{foam}}$$

The volume of a pint glass is 470 milliliters, or 0.00047 cubic meter. So the fizz factor is:

$$FF = 1 - \frac{V_{foam}}{V_{beer} + V_{foam}} = 1 - \frac{0.000037m^3}{0.00047m^3} = 0.92$$

The fizz factor directly cuts down on your swallowing speed:

$$S_{beer} = FF \times S_{drink} = 0.92 \times 0.00018\frac{m^3}{s} = 0.00017\frac{m^3}{s}$$

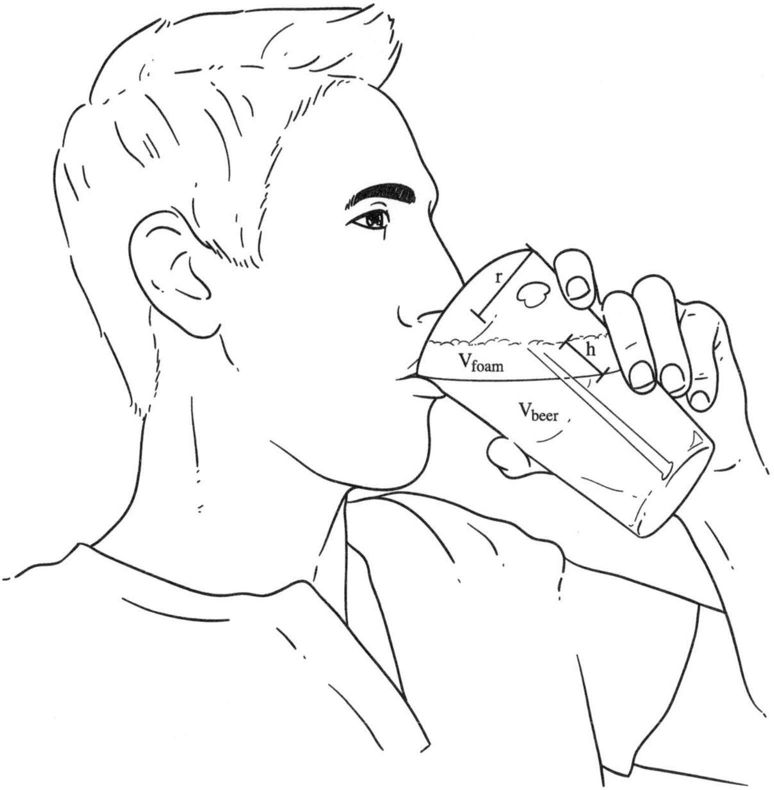
r
h
Vfoam
Vbeer

Fig. 1.i Down a Pint in One Swig

1.j POUR A DRINK LIKE TOM CRUISE
IN *COCKTAIL*

Pouring a drink out of bottles with flair is easy with Man Physics. You determine where a glass

should be relative to the bottle. The speed of exit of the liquor from the bottle is:

$$S_{pour} = \sqrt{2gh} = \sqrt{2 \times 9.8 \frac{m}{s^2} \times .14m} = 2.74 \frac{m}{s}$$

The height of the bottle above the glass is h_{glass}. So the time of flight of the liquor to the glass is:

$$t = \sqrt{\frac{2h_{glass}}{g}} = \sqrt{\frac{2 \times 0.3m}{9.8 \frac{m}{s^2}}} = 0.247s$$

This gives a total horizontal distance traveled of:

$$d = S_{pour}t = 2.74 \frac{m}{s} \times 0.247s = 0.677m$$

You want to change the height of the pour too, so you figure out the range of heights that will

still make it into the glass. Assume that for the calculations you make, the liquor enters the

center of the top of the glass and that the radius of the glass is 3.5 centimeters. Increasing the

horizontal distance by this amount gives a time of:

$$t = \frac{d}{S_{pour}} = \frac{0.712m}{2.74 \frac{m}{s}} = 0.26s$$

This gives a new height of:

$$h = \frac{1}{2}gt^2 = \frac{1}{2} \times 9.8 \frac{m}{s^2} \times 0.26^2 s^2 = 0.33m$$

Now vary your height and distance to impress and wow.

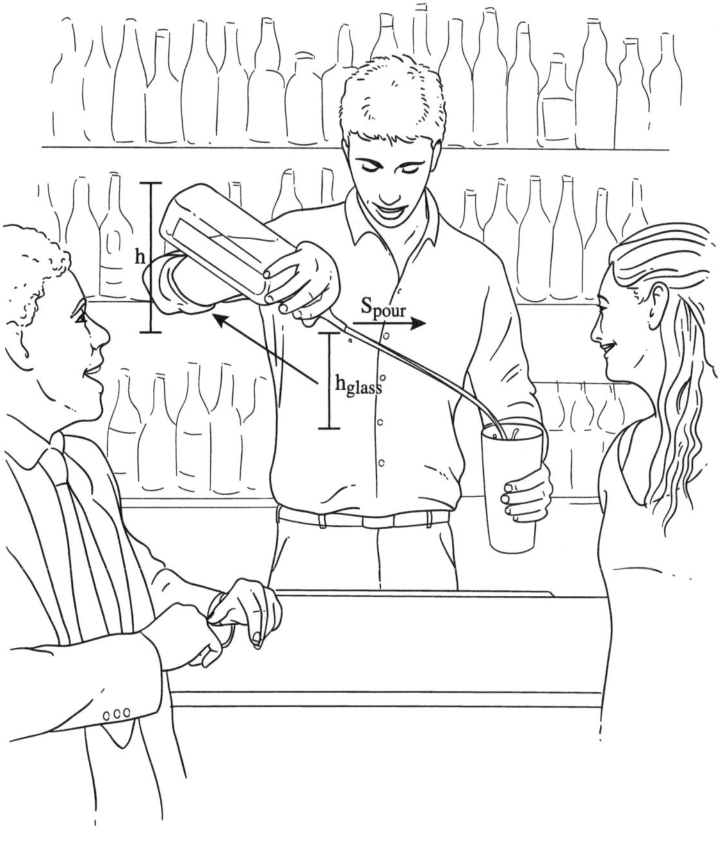
h
S_{pour}
h_{glass}

Fig. 1.j Pour a Drink like Tom Cruise in *Cocktail*

LESSONS IN THIS CHAPTER

ENTERTAINMENT

2.a CATCH A BALL IN THE STADIUM

You are enjoying a beer and a dog at the stadium when you hear the crack of the bat on the ball. You know by the sound it is a great hit. Looking up, you see that the ball is headed in your direction. You calculate on the fly that the ball will land about 2 seats to your left and 3 rows in front of you. You decide that this ball is yours. By the time you hand off your beer and dog, you estimate that you have about 2.1 seconds to make it to the catch zone. You know you can move unhindered at about 4.5 meters/second. The seats are about 1 meter across and 2 meters between. The direct line-of-site distance to the landing zone is therefore:

$$\mathrm{d} = \sqrt{\left(2.5\mathrm{d}_{\mathrm{seat}}\right)^2 + \left(3\mathrm{d}_{\mathrm{row}}\right)^2} = \sqrt{(2.5\mathrm{m})^2 + (6\mathrm{m})^2} = 6.5\mathrm{m}$$

If seats and people were not in your way, you could easily do it. The additional obstacles will slow you down. You know from your last BBQ that jumping over a lawn chair takes $^{7}/_{12}$ of a second and that you cover 2 meters. That gives a chair-hopping speed of:

$$s_{chair} = \frac{d}{t} = \frac{2m}{\frac{7}{12}s} = 3.4\frac{m}{s}$$

You have 3 seats to get over and an additional 0.5 meter to cover. The time it takes you to get there is:

$$t = 3\frac{d}{s_{chair}} + \frac{0.5m}{4.5\frac{m}{s}} = 3 \times \frac{2.0m}{3.4\frac{m}{s}} + \frac{0.5m}{4.5\frac{m}{s}} = 1.88s$$

You easily make it with enough time to get to the top of the heap of other contenders and make the catch.

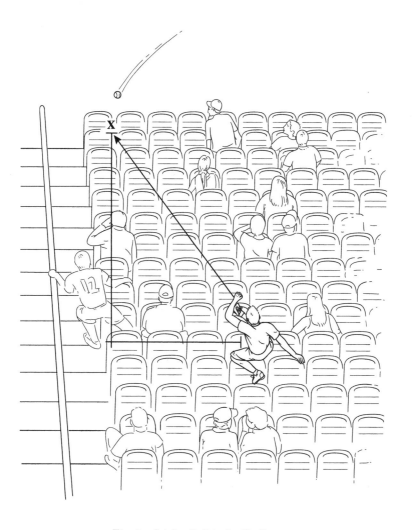

Fig. 2.a Catch a Ball in the Stadium

2.b SNEAK BACKSTAGE

You are at your favorite group's spring concert and spy an opportunity to get backstage.

Between you and rockin' out with the band is only a barrier, because the security guards ran off

to break up an inpromptu mosh pit. Calculate your chances of success if you make a go of it.

The barrier has a height of 1.4 meters. Your horizontal ground speed is 4.5 meters/second. The

distance from the barrier to the action backstage is 20 meters. To hurdle the barrier, you need a

vertical leap of 0.75 meter using your hurdling skills. The time to reach that height is:

$$t = \sqrt{\frac{2h}{g}} = \sqrt{\frac{2 \times 0.75m}{9.8\frac{m}{s^2}}} = 0.39s$$

The vertical velocity you need is:

$$v_y = gt = 9.8\frac{m}{s^2} \times 0.39s = 3.8\frac{m}{s}$$

So it takes 0.78 second for you to clear the barrier, and to cover the remaining distance, it takes:

$$t = \frac{d}{s} = \frac{20m}{4.5\frac{m}{s}} = 4.4s$$

If you want to pull this off unscathed, you'll need an exit strategy too. If the security guards

notice you rubbing elbows with the band and their cute groupies, you'll need to outrun them.

Assume they can cover about 4 meters in a second—a speed slightly slower than yours. If you

want to maximize your time with the cute band babes, figure out the minimal distance away

from you that you can safely allow the guards to reach before you take off. Your acceleration, a,

is 15 m/s^2.

h_b
d_{sec}
SECURITY

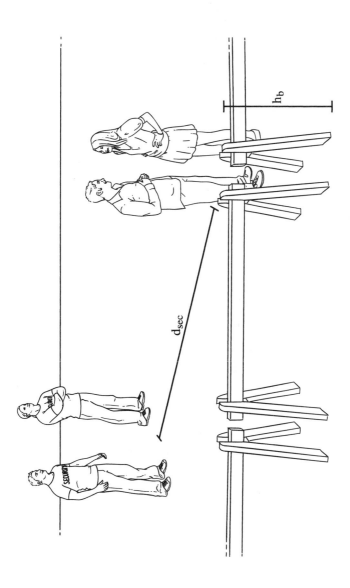

Fig. 2.b Sneak Backstage

2.c PERFECT THE BRIDGE SHUFFLE
FOR POKER NIGHT

A perfect bridge shuffle gives poker night the nostalgic flair it deserves. To do it, equilibrate the

forces involved and then let it flutter.

F_h: the force of the palm your hand

F_f: the force of friction between the cards

$F_{fingers}$: the force of your fingers

F_r: the restoring force of the card

F_t: the force of your thumbs

Assuming that you aren't going to overbend the cards, the restoring force (or Euler force) of a

card is approximately:

$$F_r = \pi^2 \frac{YI}{L^2} = \pi^2 \frac{1GPa \times 7.8 \times 10^{-14} kg \bullet m^2}{(0.088m)^2} = 0.1N$$

This value is for one card; for the deck, multiply it by 52. Determine the force that the fingers

and thumb have to exert:

$$F_{fingers} = 52 \times F_r \sin \theta - F_f$$
$$F_{fingers} = 52 \times 0.1N \sin 65 - 0.04N$$
$$F_{fingers} = 4.7N$$
$$F_t = 52 \times 0.1N \cos 65$$
$$F_t = 2.2N$$

Now, removing the force that the fingers are exerting makes the structure unstable. The

downward force of your thumbs is going to cause the bridge to collapse. As it does, move your

hands apart, and voilà! The perfect bridge shuffle.

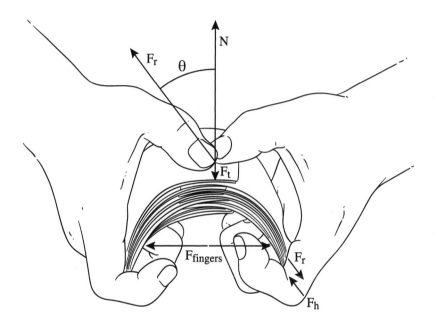

Fig. 2.c Perfect the Bridge Shuffle for Poker Night

2.d COMMAND THE DARTBOARD

The elusive bull's-eye is the goal here. You know that prowess in darts is measured by your aim for the bull. Calculate the correct velocity to release the dart so that it hits at the peak of its arc. The oche line (be careful not to step on it as you rapidly review your calculations) is a regulation 237 centimeters from the face of the dartboard, and the bull's-eye is a regulation 173 cm from the floor. You release the dart from a height of h_B = 160 cm. The time of flight is:

$$t = \sqrt{\frac{2h_g}{g}} = \sqrt{\frac{2 \times (1.73\text{m} - 1.60\text{m})}{9.8\frac{\text{m}}{\text{s}^2}}} = 0.16\text{s}$$

The horizontal speed with which you must throw is:

$$v_x = \frac{d}{t} = \frac{2.37m}{0.16s} = 17\frac{m}{s}$$

Your vertical velocity is:

$$v_y = gt = 9.8\frac{m}{s^2} \times 0.16s = 1.6\frac{m}{s}$$

Now calculate the release angle:

$$\theta = \tan^{-1}\frac{\text{v}_\text{y}}{\text{v}_\text{x}} = \tan^{-1}\frac{1.6\frac{\text{m}}{\text{s}}}{17\frac{\text{m}}{\text{s}}} = 5.4^\circ$$

Finally, you need to know your initial release speed:

$$v = \sqrt{v_x^2 + v_y^2} = \sqrt{\left(17\frac{m}{s}\right)^2 + \left(1.6\frac{m}{s}\right)^2} = 17.1\frac{m}{s}$$

Using these values, you make shooting the bull look easy. Your buds will always want you on their team come dart night.

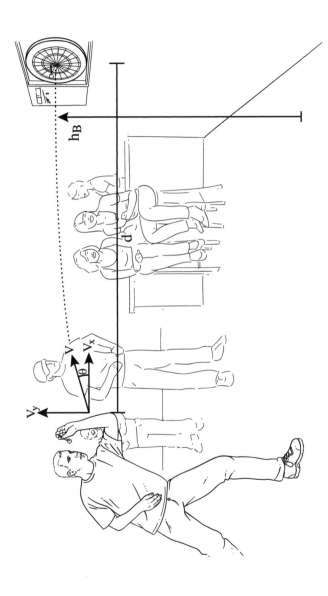

Fig. 2.d Command the Dartboard

2.e WIN AT QUARTERS

You know that drinking games prove something. You're not sure exactly what, but you just know that you want to be good at it. Bringing your Man Physics to bear on the problem, you figure out the perfect quarters shot. You decide that due to the symmetry of the round edge of the quarter, it makes the most sense to bounce directly off this. You figure that the quarter will lose about 1/3 of its energy on the bounce. You find the energy you need to provide for the quarter to reach a maximum height of h_{cup} + 6 centimeters.

$$E_v = 3 \times mg\left(h_{cup} + 0.06cm\right) = 3 \times 0.006kg \times 9.8\frac{m}{s^2}(0.12m + 0.06m) = 0.03J$$

This gives an initial vertical speed of:

$$v_y = \sqrt{\frac{\frac{2E_v}{3}}{m}} = \sqrt{\frac{\frac{2 \times 0.03J}{3}}{0.006kg}} = 1.8\frac{m}{s}$$

The time it takes to reach the max height is:

$$t_m = \frac{v_y}{g} = \frac{1.8\frac{m}{s}}{9.8\frac{m}{s^2}} = 0.18s$$

The total time of flight from the bounce to the opening of the cup is:

$$t = \sqrt{\frac{2 \times .06m}{9.8\frac{m}{s^2}}} + t_m = 0.11s + 0.18s = 0.29s$$

For the cup a distance of 0.28 meter from the bounce, the initial horizontal velocity is:

$$v_x = \frac{d}{t} = \frac{0.28m}{0.29s} = 0.97\frac{m}{s}$$

Reflection. So you release the quarter with an angle of:

$$\theta = \tan^{-1}\frac{v_y}{v_x} = \tan^{-1}\frac{1.8\frac{m}{s}}{0.97\frac{m}{s}} = 61.7°$$

You sink the quarter and are damn proud of it!

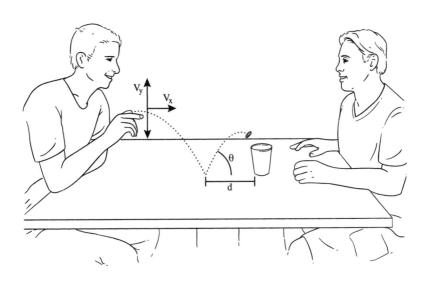

Fig. 2.e Win at Quarters

2.f WALK HOME DRUNK
WITHOUT FALLING OVER

The drunken spins are no laughing matter. Well, maybe they are, but to navigate a walk back home after your night out isn't. You need to determine how your steps are influenced by the head spins. First, determine the rate of spinning of the world. You note that it takes about 0.1 second for things to move across about 1/6 of your peripheral vision. This gives an angular rate of:

$$\omega = \frac{\theta}{t} = \frac{\frac{1}{6} \times 180°}{0.3s} = \frac{100°}{s}$$

The direction of your steps need to make up for this perceived spinning. You calculate what the direction your step must be considering that the time to take a drunken step is 0.73 second.

$$\theta = \omega t = \frac{100°}{s} \times 0.73s = 73°$$

So to counteract the spinning, you have to feel like you are making your steps at an angle of 73° to the direction you normally step and opposite the direction of spinning. Now you can walk a straight line. Note that your foot will not really have to move out away from your body at a 73° angle.

To outside observers, you will appear to be walking a normal straight line. However, you yourself will feel like you are stepping out away from your body at an odd angle. This is a typical example of Man Physics relativity.

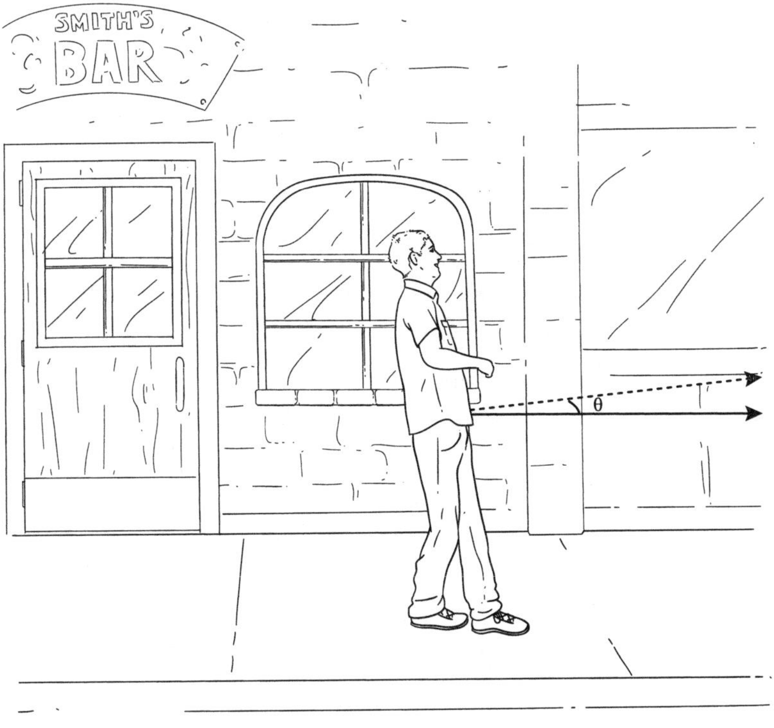
SMITH'S
BAR
θ

Fig. 2.f Walk Home Drunk Without Falling Over

2.g DO A KEGSTAND

Ah, the kegstand. Typical party stuff for guys. You know that the steeper the angle, the better you look. So you figure out the max angle at which you will be able to do a kegstand based on your swallowing speed while lying down, 0.16 liter/second (l/s). Knowing that as you get elevated, your swallowing speed will slow down as a consequence of the extra swallowing energy it takes to overcome gravity. The equation for slowed drinking speed is:

$$S_{drink} = S_{lying} \cos \frac{2\alpha}{3}$$

The flow coming out of the tap is S_{tap} = 0.1 liter/second. Your drinking speed must not drop below the flow coming out of the tap, or else things get sloppy. To find the maximum angle you can get elevated, you plug in and solve for α:

$$S_{drink} = S_{tap}$$

$$S_{tap} = S_{lying} \cos \frac{2\alpha}{3}$$

$$\alpha = \frac{3}{2} \cos^{-1} \frac{S_{tap}}{S_{lying}} = \frac{3}{2} \cos^{-1} \frac{0.1 \frac{l}{s}}{0.16 \frac{l}{s}} = 43°$$

Not too shabby! Just remember to kick out when you've proved that you are king of the kegstand.

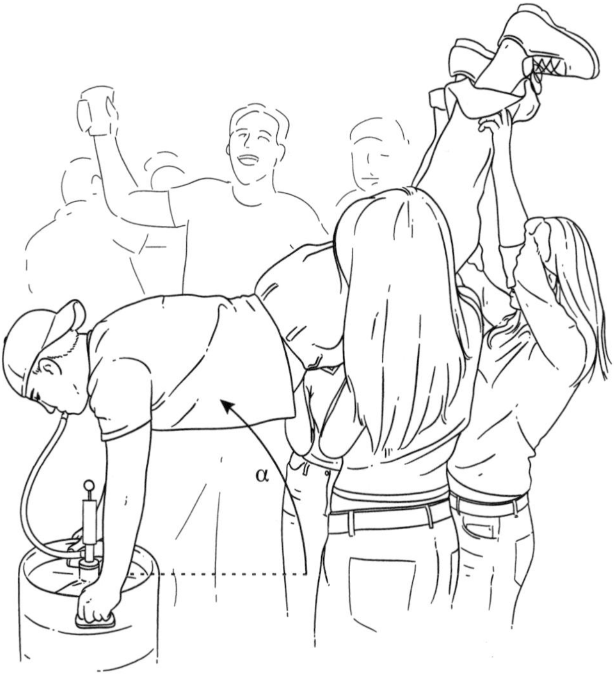
α

Fig. 2.g Do a Kegstand

2.h PROPERLY SHOTGUN A BEER

Properly shotgunning a beer requires some quick moves and serious sprint drinking. Once the can is punctured, the residual pressure will force some of the beer out. This is the spout. (Extra points for not losing any of the spout on the ground!) The beer is going to flow fastest right after the can is opened. Calculate the initial flow coming out of the can to know how fast you have to start swallowing. The speed of liquid leaving the can is:

$$S_{shotgun} = \sqrt{2gh} = \sqrt{2 \times 9.8 \frac{m}{s^2} \times 0.09m} = 1.8 \frac{m}{s}$$

The radius of the hole you created in the can is 0.003 meter. So the area of the hole is:

$$A = \pi r^2 = \pi \times (0.003m)^2 = 2.8 \times 10^{-5} m^2$$

The initial flow coming out of the can, in liters per second, will be:

$$F_{init} = S_{shotgun} A = 0.00005 \frac{m^3}{s} \times \frac{1000l}{m^3} = 0.05 \frac{l}{s}$$

Your upright swallowing speed is much greater than this. So you can add some suction to outperform the other slugs who are also shotgunning.

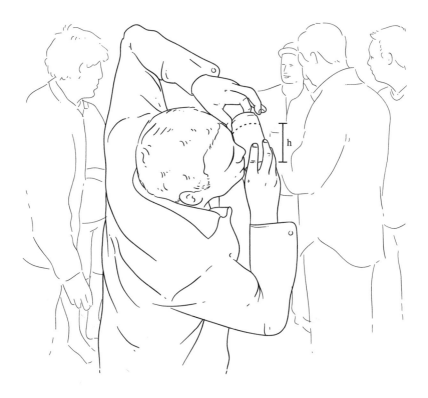

Fig. 2.h Properly Shotgun a Beer

2.i NAVIGATE A CROWDED BAR
WITH MULTIPLE DRINKS

Getting through a crowded bar with drinks in hand is as much an art as it is a challenge. Most of you know about Brownian motion, but when it comes to navigating a bar, the Man Physics concept is called *Bar*nian motion. The key to this is the collision factor.

A few important things to consider: how thirsty your buds are for the drinks you're carrying, the possibility of spillage along your path, and the chance of "colliding" with cute girls along the way. Take these into account by calculating the average distance between "collisions":

$$l = \tau v$$

Here τ is the mean time between occasions of running into another person, and v is the average speed of motion in the bar. You also apply the equation for the collision factor C when you move a distance dx:

$$C = \sigma n dx$$

The number of people between you and where you want to get with your drinks, divided by the length of the path, is n. The collision cross section, σ, is important. The fortunate thing for men everywhere is that chicks that you really want to "collide" with naturally have small σ's. Dudes have high σ's. Using the equations above and your Man Physics freedom of expression, you determine that the equation to solve for your path is:

$$P = L_T \sum_N C_i$$

L_T is the total path length. Perusing this equation for a while and thinking about the situation, you realize that the physics involved only points to one solution: You take the path with the greatest number of girls in it. One complication arises because of this: You may never get back to the friends who sent you out for the drinks. But you know that this is always a risk that you have to take—and let's face it, they knew it too. The upside is that right there in your hands are the drinks that will sustain you in your Barnian motion.

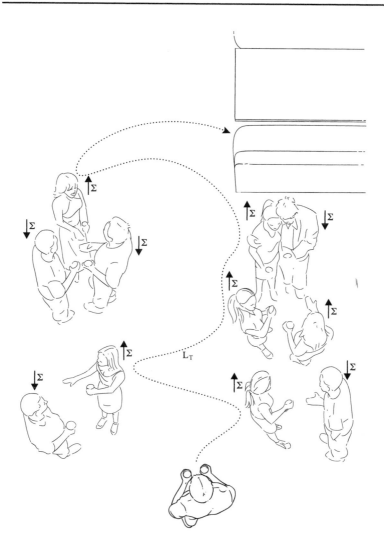

Fig. 2.i Navigate a Crowded Bar with Multiple Drinks

2.j SHOOT THE PERFECT BEIRUT SHOT

Shooting a Beirut shot is very similar to a shot in quarters. The major difference is the distance

of the throw and the height of release. You calculate the time for an h_{cup} + 10 cm height of the

bounce, using conservation of energy and equations for projectile motion:

$$v_y = \sqrt{2g\left(h_{cup} + 0.1m\right)}$$

$$h_{cup} = -\frac{1}{2}gt_b^2 + v_y t_b$$

$$h_{cup} = -\frac{1}{2}gt_b^2 + \sqrt{2g\left(h_{cup} + 0.1m\right)}t_b$$

$$t_b = \frac{\sqrt{2g\left(h_{cup} + 0.1m\right)} \pm \sqrt{2g\left(h_{cup} + 0.1m\right) - 2gh_{cup}}}{g}$$

For h_{cup} = 0.12 meter, this gives times of:

$$t_b = \frac{\sqrt{2\times 9.8\frac{m}{s^2}\left(0.12m + 0.1m\right)} \pm \sqrt{2\times 9.8\frac{m}{s^2}\left(0.12m + 0.1m\right) - 2\times 9.8\frac{m}{s^2}\times 0.12m}}{9.8\frac{m}{s^2}}$$

$$t_b = 0.212 \pm 0.143$$

Take the longer of the two times, since that corresponds to the ball at the cup. So t_b = 0.355.

Find the time it takes the ball to hit the table after release:

$$t_r = \sqrt{\frac{2h_o}{g}} = \sqrt{\frac{2\times 3\left(h_{cup} + 0.1m\right)}{g}} = \sqrt{\frac{2\times 0.66m}{9.8\frac{m}{s^2}}} = 0.135s$$

The total time it takes the ball to reach the cup is:

$$t = t_r + t_b = 0.135s + 0.355s = 0.49s$$

The total distance it must travel is 1.7 meters. So you throw the ball with an initial velocity of:

$$v_x = \frac{d}{t} = \frac{1.7m}{0.49s} = 3.5\frac{m}{s}$$

The shot is sunk! Wash that ball for the next one.

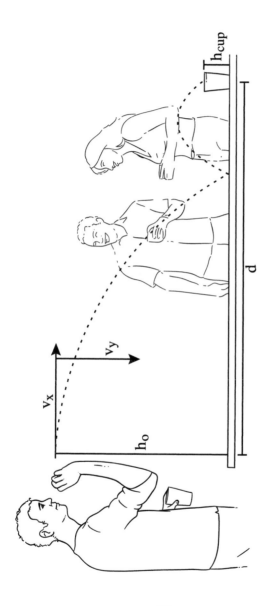

Fig. 2.j Shoot the Perfect Beirut Shot

LESSONS IN THIS CHAPTER

SPORTS

3.a ACE A TENNIS SERVE

The shear pleasure of hauling off and serving up an ace on the tennis court is worthy of a Man Physics calculation. Determine the ultimate flat serve that just clears the net. At the center, the net is 0.914 meter high. You hit the ball from an initial height of 3.2 meters. Calculate the vertical downward speed and angle of the hit for a horizontal speed of 20 meters/second. The time it takes to travel to the net is thus:

$$t = \frac{d}{v_x} = \frac{11.9m}{20\frac{m}{s}} = 0.6s$$

Calculate the initial downward speed:

$$v_{0y} = \frac{(h_{net} + r_{ball}) - h_{serve} + \frac{1}{2}gt^2}{t} = \frac{0.918m - 3.2m + \frac{1}{2} \times 9.8\frac{m}{s^2} \times (0.6s)^2}{0.6s} = -0.91\frac{m}{s}$$

Check to make sure your serve will not be a fault. To remain good, it must not travel farther than 6.4 meters horizontally after crossing the net. Calculate the time it takes to hit the ground from the net. The downward speed at the net is

$$v_y = v_{0y} + gt = 0.91\frac{m}{s} + 9.8\frac{m}{s^2} \times 0.6s = 6.8\frac{m}{s}$$

The final downward velocity is:

$$v_{fy} = \sqrt{v_y^2 + 2gh_{net}} = \sqrt{\left(6.8\frac{m}{s}\right)^2 + 2 \times 9.8\frac{m}{s^2} \times 0.914m} = 8.0\frac{m}{s}$$

The time it takes is:

$$t = \frac{v_{fy} - v_y}{g} = \frac{8.0\frac{m}{s} - 6.8\frac{m}{s}}{9.8\frac{m}{s^2}} = 0.12s$$

$$d = v_x t = 20 \frac{m}{s} \times 0.12m = 2.5m$$

Finally, find the angle of the ball coming off the racquet:

$$\theta = \tan^{-1} \frac{v_{0y}}{v_x} = \tan^{-1} \frac{0.91 \frac{m}{s}}{20 \frac{m}{s}} = 2.6°$$

And the serve is good! Got to love physics.

v_x
v_y
h_{serve}
h_{net}

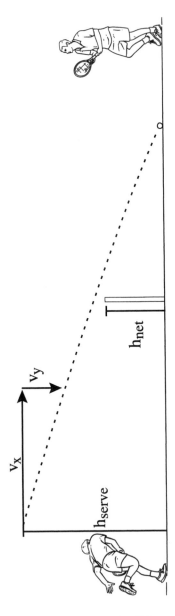

Fig. 3.a Ace a Tennis Serve

3.b PERFECT THE POOL BREAK

Beer and babes aside, a good game of eight-ball can make the night, and the break definitely

sets the mood for the game. It is almost like psychological warfare. You can break with

confidence, make the cue ball roll to the perfect starting spot, and put your opponent on the

defensive from the start. The key is a tight rack and getting the cue ball to the object balls with

the greatest energy. Assume you are dealing with elastic collisions. Because of conservation of

momentum, you know that the cue will recoil from the break. You determine the much-

overlooked effect of spin on the cue after the initial collision. The cue has a speed of v when it

hits. The recoil velocity is:

$$v_r = \frac{m_c - M}{m_c + M} v$$

M is the effective mass of the rack, which you take to be $2m_c$, assuming some slop in the rack;

and m_c = 170 grams is the mass of the cue. So v_r is:

$$v_r = \frac{m_c - M}{m_c + M} v = \frac{-1m_c}{3m_c} v = -\frac{1}{3} v$$

To leave the cue close to the foot spot on the table, you need to provide topspin to counteract

recoil. To find out how much, you first calculate how far the ball recoils. The coefficient of

kinetic friction between the ball and table is μ = 0.2. The ball will move back a distance of:

$$d = \frac{\frac{1}{2} m_c v_r^2}{N\mu} = \frac{m_c v_r^2}{2 m_c g \mu} = \frac{v_r^2}{2 g \mu} = \frac{v^2}{2 g \mu 3^2}$$

Take v = 4 meters/second for a good break, and this gives:

$$d = \frac{v_r^2}{2 g \mu} = \frac{4^2}{2 \times 9.8 \frac{m}{s^2} \times 0.2 \times 9} = 0.45m$$

after the ball recoils a distance d. The moment of inertia of the ball is $I = 2m_c r^2 / 5$.

$$\omega_f = \sqrt{\omega^2 - \frac{2m_c \mu d}{I}}$$

The radius of the ball is $r = 2.85$ centimeters. For a topspin of $v/2$, this gives:

$$\omega_f = \sqrt{\left(\frac{v}{2r}\right)^2 - \frac{5\mu d}{r^2}} = \sqrt{\left(\frac{2\frac{m}{s}}{0.0285m}\right)^2 - \frac{5 \times 0.2 \times 0.45m}{(0.0285m)^2}} = 66.1\frac{rad}{s}$$

Thus you have some spin to bring the ball back toward the center of the table. Great control of

the cue ball. Now you can run the table!

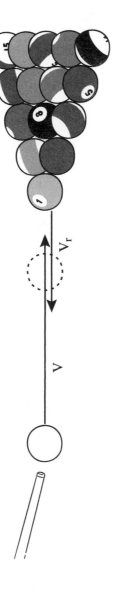

Fig. 3.b Perfect the Pool Break

3.c LAUNCH A SMOOTH-SAILING FRISBEE

You are enjoying a day at the beach when your honey wants to play Frisbee. So you put down your beer and apply some physics to throwing a Frisbee. The application of Newton's Second Law tells you how to balance out the forces. For a Frisbee, these forces are:

F_l: lift force

F_d: drag force

F_w: weight

A Frisbee with aerodymanic constants $C_D = 0.1$, $C_l = 0.2$, $v = 13$ m/s, $\alpha = 10°$, $r = 0.25$ meter, $A = \pi r^2$, $\rho = 1.23$ kg/m^3, and $m = 0.12$ kg produces forces at launch of:

$$F_l = \frac{\rho v^2 A C_l}{2} = \frac{1.23\frac{kg}{m^3}\left(13\frac{m}{s}\right)^2 \times 0.196m^2 \times 0.2}{2} = 4.08N$$

$$F_d = \frac{\rho v^2 A C_d}{2} = \frac{1.23\frac{kg}{m^3}\left(13\frac{m}{s}\right)^2 \times 0.196m^2 \times 0.1}{2} = 2.04N$$

$$F_w = mg = 0.12kg \times 9.8\frac{m}{s^s} = 1.18N$$

Since F_w is located at the center of mass and the other forces are not, there is a torque that the Frisbee experiences. For the smoothest flight, you need to produce a nice angular momentum that will work against the torque. The angular momentum of the Frisbee is produced by the flick of your wrist. You produce an angular velocity of 13 rad/s. This gives the Frisbee an angular momentum of:

$$\mathrm{L} = \mathrm{I}\omega = \frac{\mathrm{mr}^2\omega}{2} = \frac{0.12\mathrm{kg}(0.25\mathrm{m})^2 13\frac{\mathrm{rad}}{\mathrm{s}}}{2} = 0.05\frac{\mathrm{kg}\times\mathrm{m}^2}{\mathrm{s}}$$

This creates the perfect counter-torque to give the Frisbee the float that will totally impress your honey.

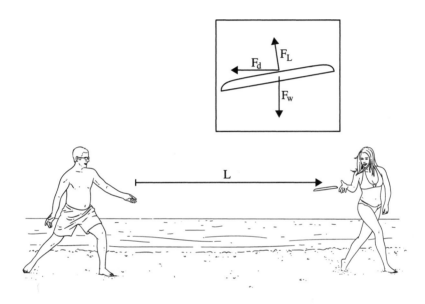

Fig. 3.c Launch a Smooth-Sailing Frisbee

3.d EXECUTE A FLAWLESS LAYUP

This shot is going to be all net. Apply the equations of projectile motion twice: once for you and then again for the ball. You approach the hoop and jump with v = 3.57 meters/second (like a 357 Magnum) at an angle of 73.7° (like a Boeing 737) to the horizontal and a distance of 0.688 meter from the hoop. You calculate your v_y and v_x:

$$v_y = v \sin \theta_j = 3.57 \frac{m}{s} \sin 73.7° = 3.43 \frac{m}{s}$$

$$v_x = v \cos \theta_j = 3.57 \frac{m}{s} \cos 73.7° = 1.00 \frac{m}{s}$$

With these values, you find your vertical leap:

$$h_{leap} = \frac{v_y^2}{2g} = \frac{\left(3.43 \frac{m}{s}\right)^2}{2 \times 9.8 \frac{m}{s^2}} = 0.6m$$

To get to this height, it takes:

$$t_{leap} = \sqrt{\frac{2h_{leap}}{g}} = \sqrt{\frac{2 \times 0.6m}{9.8 \frac{m}{s^2}}} = 0.35s$$

You have traveled 0.35 meter in this time. At the apex of your jump, you release the ball with outstretched arm. You take into consideration the 0.119-meter radius of the ball and realize that, to make it just clear the rim, you need to get it to an additional height of 0.56 meter. Your horizontal velocity is still 1 meter/second. Find the v_{yball} that you need to make the shot:

$$v_{yball} = \sqrt{2gh} = \sqrt{2 \times 9.8 \frac{m}{s^2} \times 0.56m} = 3.31 \frac{m}{s}$$

Because you've given the ball this vertical speed, the shot drops. But then, you already knew it would.

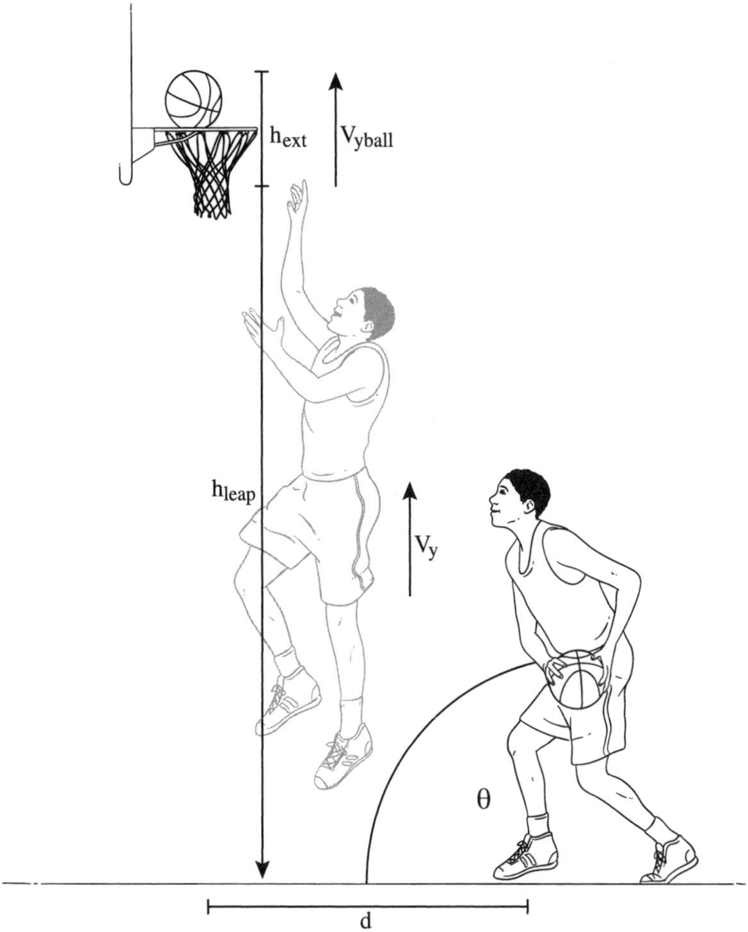
h_{ext}
V_{yball}
h_{leap}
V_y
θ
d

Fig. 3.d Execute a Flawless Layup

3.e SOAK SUNBATHERS
WITH A MONSTER CANNONBALL

Your mission for the day is to totally drench someone. It's so hot out, and all the unsuspecting sunbathers are just asking for it. Plus you love to hear the women scream. You determine how to create the biggest splash. The important consideration is the value of S_{plash}. It will tell you where along the pool to perform the maneuver. You calculate it as:

$$S_{plash} = \sum_i \frac{B_i}{r_{Bi}^2}$$

The distance away from your entrance point of the sunbathers is r_B. B_i is the desire term for the ith bozo that you want to get with the splash. It is found with the equation:

$$B = H_F + R_F$$

H_F is the hotness factor, and R_F is the revenge factor, for each individual splashee. Both are on a scale of 1 to 10. Calculate S_{plash} for the given layout at the pool. There are two obvious entrance points. For the first one:

$B_1 = 8 + 0$

$r_{B1} = 0.1$ meter

$B_2 = 2 + 5$

$r_{B2} = 1.3$ meters

$B_3 = 0 + 1$

$r_{B3} = 2$ meters

So:

$$S_{plash} = \frac{8}{(0.1m)^2} + \frac{7}{(1.3m)^2} + \frac{1}{(2.0m)^2} = \frac{800}{m^2} + \frac{4.1}{m^2} + \frac{0.25}{m^2} = \frac{804.35}{m^2}$$

$B_1 = 0 + 4$

$r_{B1} = 0.5$ meter

$B_2 = 7 + 5$

$r_{B2} = 0.7$ meter

So:

$$S_{plash} = \frac{4}{(0.5\text{m})^2} + \frac{17}{(0.7\text{m})^2} = \frac{50.7}{\text{m}^2}$$

You pick the first entrance point. To create the largest splash, you need to hit the water with the greatest energy. To do this, you determine the horizontal speed you will need to just clear your butt from hitting the edge of the pool and add a little for splash release. For a jump speed of 5 meters/second, and a butt-clearing distance of 0.7 meter, find the jump angle by solving for ϑ:

$$\cos^4\theta - \cos^2\theta + \frac{g^2d^2}{4v^4} = 0$$

$$\theta = \cos^{-1}\left(\sqrt{\frac{1 \pm \sqrt{1 - \frac{g^2d^2}{4v^4}}}{2}}\right) = \cos^{-1}\left(\sqrt{\frac{1 \pm \sqrt{1 - \frac{\left(9.8\frac{\text{m}}{\text{s}^2}\right)^2 (0.8\text{m})^2}{4\left(5\frac{\text{m}}{\text{s}}\right)^4}}}{2}}\right) = \cos^{-1}\left(\sqrt{\frac{1 \pm 0.98763}{2}}\right)$$

Taking the minus sign above, you get a jump angle of $\vartheta = 85.5^\circ$ giving you the correct horizontal speed. You have accomplished your mission for the day.

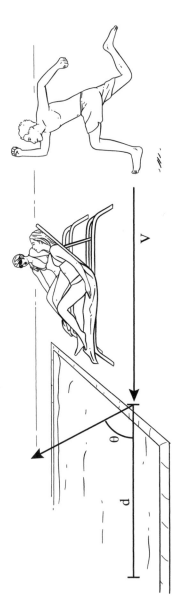

Fig. 3.e Soak Sunbathers with a Monster Cannonball

3.f CATCH A FISH

You already know how to fillet a fish with style (see Fillet a Fish). Now to catch it. There is a light

wind of 3 knots blowing out of the northwest. You are casting for a patch of promising lily pads

offshore about 13 meters due south. You find the position along the shore from which you need

to cast to take the wind into account. You find this for a horizontal casting speed of 7

meters/second due south. Find the time it takes the lure to travel 13 meters:

$$t = \frac{d}{v_{cast} + v_{wind} \sin\theta_{wind}} = \frac{13m}{7\frac{m}{s} + 3kn \times \frac{0.514\frac{m}{s}}{kn} \times \sin 45°} = 1.6s$$

Calculate the distance to the east that the lure will get blown:

$$d = v_{wind} \cos\theta_{wind} t = 3kn \times \frac{0.514\frac{m}{s}}{kn} \times \cos 45° \times 1.6s = 1.7m$$

Since the lure gets blown 1.7 meters to the east, you will move along the shore 1.7 meters to

the west of the direct-line cast. Simple when Man Physics shows you how!

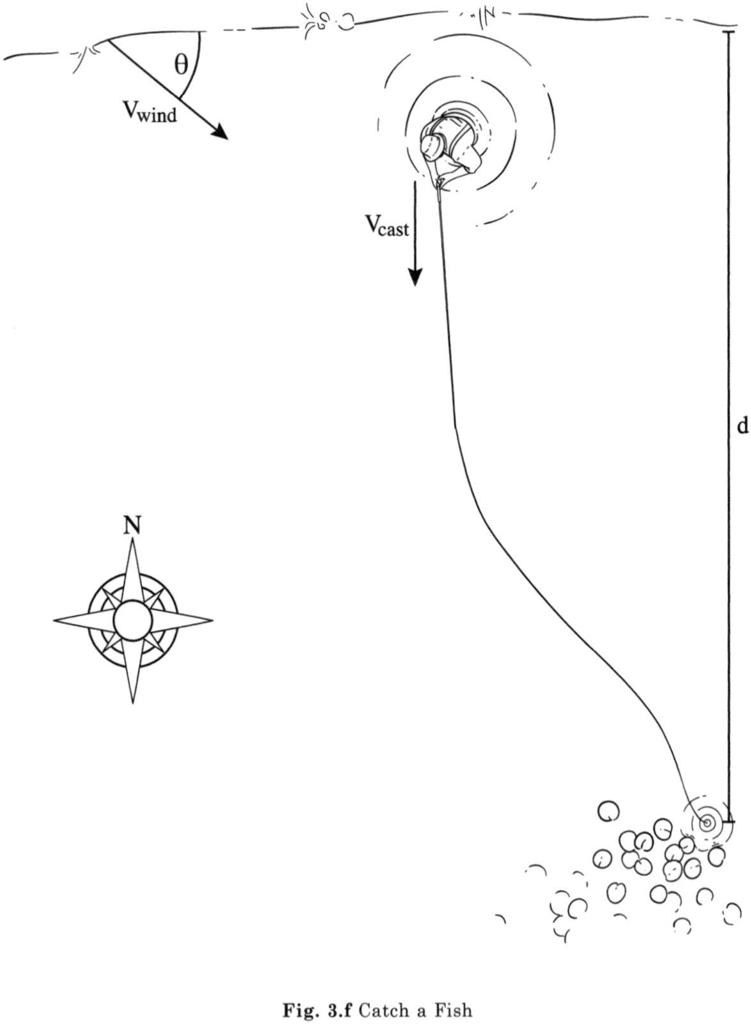
θ
Vwind
Vcast
d
N

Fig. 3.f Catch a Fish

3.g PADDLE A CANOE

You are out on a canoe trip with some buds and pull off for a rest. A group of girls tubing down the river just landed on the opposite bank. They shout over, asking if you guys want to join them for lunch. No question about that! Your buds in the other canoe start to paddle straight across to them. You, though, realize that the fastest way across may not be the most direct way. The current is moving at about 4 meters/second. You know that the paddling speed of the canoe has been about 7 m/s without the current. You and your crewmate can carry the canoe on land at a speed of 5 m/s. The distance across the river is 50 m. Thinking quickly, you determine the fastest way to get across. Calculate the time to paddle straight across, accounting for the current:

$$t_1 = \frac{d}{v_{paddle} - v_{current}} = \frac{50m}{3\frac{m}{s}} = 16.7s$$

Calculate the time it takes to carry the canoe upstream and then paddle directly across, allowing the current to take care of the downstream component of your vector of travel:

$$t_2 = \frac{d}{v_{paddle}} + \frac{\frac{d}{v_{paddle}}v_{current}}{v_{carry}} = \frac{d}{v_{paddle}}\left(1 + \frac{v_{current}}{v_{carry}}\right) = \frac{50m}{7\frac{m}{s}}\left(1 + \frac{4\frac{m}{s}}{5\frac{m}{s}}\right) = 12.9s$$

Comparing these two times convinces your friend to carry upstream. Calculate the distance you need to carry:

$$d_{carry} = v_{current}\frac{d}{v_{paddle}} = 4\frac{m}{s} \times \frac{50m}{7\frac{m}{s}} = 28.9m$$

The ladies will wonder exactly what you are doing, but when you get there first, they'll think you performed some kind of river god magic.

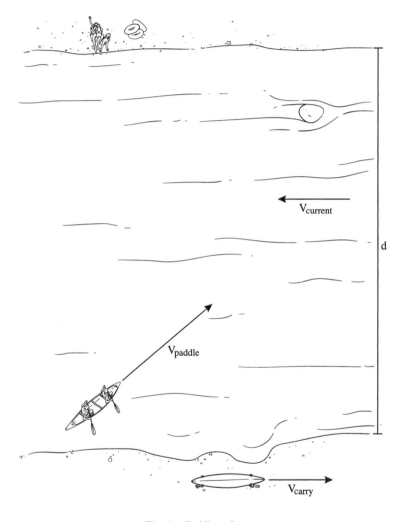

$V_{current}$

d

V_{paddle}

V_{carry}

Fig. 3.g Paddle a Canoe

3.h PITCH A KNUCKLEBALL

Knuckleball! Enough said. To pitch it, you must make the ball leave your hand with (ideally) no spin. Accomplish this by gripping the ball with your fingertips and fingers contracted. Calculate the time to extend and release the pitch. Assume that the thumb is always going to be the first to reach full extension. If it has an acceleration of 3 m/s^2, then the time to release is:

$$t = \sqrt{\frac{2l_{thumb}}{a_t}} = \sqrt{\frac{2 \times 0.06m}{3\frac{m}{s^2}}} = 0.2s$$

Before this time, the fingers are providing the forces on the ball that keep it in rotational equilibrium. Calculate the force that each finger must exert on the ball during this time:

$$F = ma = 0.145kg \times 3\frac{m}{s^2} = 0.4N$$

So if you are pitching the three-finger knuckler, then each finger must exert an additional force of 0.145 newton (N) in the direction of release during the finger extension.

Assuming that all fingers release at the same time, you will have a knuckleball on its squirrely way to striking out the batter.

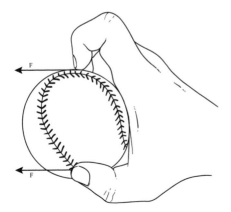

Fig. 3.h Pitch a Knuckleball

3.i GET OUT OF A SAND TRAP

How did sand traps ever become part of a golf course anyhow? You can ponder that at the

clubhouse. For now, you need to get out of one and make it 8 meters to the flag. You use the

momentum of your club to create an explosion of sand that will carry your ball out of the trap

and onto the green. For a swing speed of s_{wing} = 16 meters/second and the weight of the head of

the club m_c = 0.5 kilogram, the momentum is:

$$p_{swing} = m_c s_{wing} = 0.5kg \times 16\frac{m}{s} = 8\frac{kg \times m}{s}$$

You hit behind the ball with an open face on the sand wedge. This creates a momentum wave

through the sand that lifts the ball, provides the trajectory, and gives it some backspin.

Assuming that the average momentum given to the sand is 7.4 kg × m/s, the ball then gets a

momentum of:

$$p_{ball} = p_{swing} - p_{sand} = m_c s_{wing} = 8\frac{kg \times m}{s} - 7.4\frac{kg \times m}{s} = 0.6\frac{kg \times m}{s}$$

The speed of the ball is then:

$$v_{ball} = \frac{p_{ball}}{m_{ball}} = \frac{0.6\frac{kg \times m}{s}}{0.046kg} = 13\frac{m}{s}$$

The face of the sand wedge is angled at 33°, so the ball's launch angle is 90° − 33° = 57°, giving a

range of the shot of:

$$d = v\cos\theta\sqrt{\frac{(v\sin\theta)^2}{g^2}} = 13\frac{m}{s}\cos 57°\sqrt{\frac{\left(13\frac{m}{s}\sin 57°\right)^2}{\left(9.8\frac{m}{s^2}\right)^2}} = 7.9m$$

Perfect! Now putt that baby in!

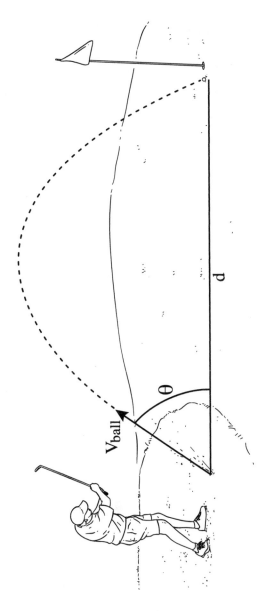

Fig. 3.i Get Out of a Sand Trap

3.j SPIN A BASKETBALL ON YOUR FINGERTIP

Download the theme music for the Globetrotters for this one! Spinning the ball as fast as you can and keeping the axis of rotation vertical on the toss up are ultimately important. Determine the maximum angular momentum you give the basketball. First determine the maximum acceleration you can achieve. Calculate the force of static friction on the fingertips:

$$f = N\mu = mg\mu = 0.624kg \times 9.8\frac{m}{s^2} \times .5 = 3.1N$$

Now find the linear acceleration:

$$a = \frac{f}{m} = g\mu = 9.8\frac{m}{s^2} \times .5 = 4.9\frac{m}{s^2}$$

Assuming that you apply this linear acceleration tangentially at r = 0.07 meter about a consistent axis of rotation, the angular acceleration is:

$$\alpha = \frac{a}{r} = \frac{4.9\frac{m}{s^2}}{0.07m} = 70\frac{rad}{s^2}$$

Applying this over $\Delta\vartheta$ = 189°, you attain a maximum angular velocity of:

$$\omega = \sqrt{2\alpha\Delta\theta} = \sqrt{2 \times 70\frac{rad}{s^2} \times 189° \times \frac{\pi}{180°}} = 21\frac{rad}{s}$$

That's totally maxing it out! Now, upon catching the ball, you simply make certain that your finger is in the center of the ball and on the axis of rotation.

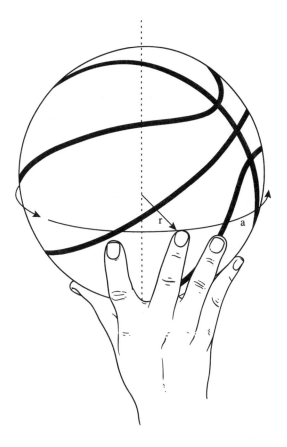

Fig. 3.j Spin a Basketball on Your Fingertip

3.k HIT TO THE OPPOSITE FIELD

You see the fielder sleeping out there and know that is where to put the ball. You step up to the plate, take some warm-up swings, and ready yourself for this split-second calculation. Assuming you hit to the field at your back, to hit to the opposite field, you time your swing a little bit later. Take the speed of the pitch to be v_p, your swing acceleration $\alpha_s = 58$ rad/s^2, and the angle through which the bat accelerates for your natural hit is $\vartheta_1 = 278°$, or 4.85 rad. The time it takes to make the natural swing is:

$$t_1 = \sqrt{\frac{2\theta_1}{\alpha_s}}$$

To hit to the opposite field, decrease ϑ_1 by 45°, or 0.785 rad. This gives the opposite-field swing time as:

$$t_2 = \sqrt{\frac{2(\theta_1 - 0.785 rad)}{\alpha_s}}$$

Thus the difference in swing time is:

$$\Delta t = t_1 - t_2 = \sqrt{\frac{2\theta_1}{\alpha_s}} - \sqrt{\frac{2(\theta_1 - 0.785 rad)}{\alpha_s}} = \sqrt{\frac{2\theta_1}{\alpha_s}} - \sqrt{\frac{2(\theta_1 - 0.785 rad)}{\alpha_s}}$$

So you exercise the ultimate in restraint and hold off your swing for an additional time:

$$\Delta t = \sqrt{\frac{2 \times 4.85 rad}{58\frac{rad}{s^2}}} - \sqrt{\frac{2(4.85 rad - 0.785 rad)}{58\frac{rad}{s^2}}} = 0.41s - 0.37s = 0.04s$$

This four-hundreths of a second lag in your initial swing start gets the ball past that sleeping outfielder.

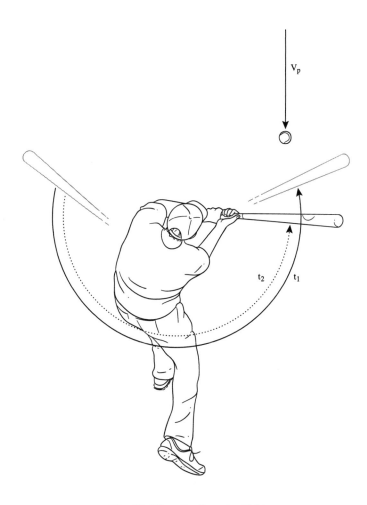

Fig. 3.k Hit to the Opposite Field

LESSONS IN THIS CHAPTER

AROUND
THE HOUSE

4.a GET OUT OF TAKING OUT THE GARBAGE

There is more than one way to skin a cat. In this case, the effort of taking out the garbage is a

waste of energy, since you can just push it down right where it is and save a trip outside. You

figure out the downward pressure required to be a human trash compactor. For everyday trash

items, you estimate the average pressure of failure:

Milk carton = 12.5 pascals (Pa)

Egg carton = 10.3 Pa

Vegetable matter = 13.0 Pa

Candy wrappers, potato chip bags, and plastic wrap = 3 Pa

For a random selection of these items on the same level in the trash can, you add the pressures:

$$P_L = 12.5kPa + (0.5 \times 13.0kPa) + (50 \times 3kPa) = 169Pa$$

And for four of these representative levels:

$$P_T = 4P_L = (4 \times 169Pa) = 676Pa$$

Figure out the pressure that an 80-kg man can exert pushing down with his whole weight with

one hand. Take the area of the hand to be 15 cm × 8 cm. Then:

$$P_M = \frac{F_{body}}{A_{hand}} = \frac{mg}{A_{hand}} = \frac{80kg \times 9.8\frac{m}{s^2}}{0.15m \times 0.08m} = 65,300Pa$$

Obviously, doing a one-handed handstand on the garbage is a bit of overkill. The utility of Man

Physics shows through once more. No trip outside necessary.

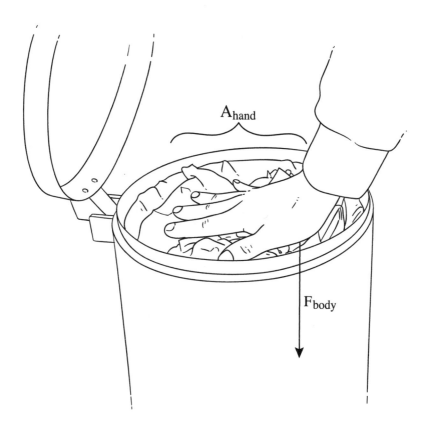

Fig. 4.a Get Out of Taking Out the Garbage

4.b GET OUT OF PAINTING THE BEDROOM

You know the paint in the bedroom is perfectly good, but your attempts to explain this fall on deaf ears. Now it is time to get serious. You break out the big guns: Man Physics. You convince yourself that you remember reading somewhere that Dr. Dooless performed experiments to determine the energy expenditure required for effective painting of bedroom walls. In his research, he determined that the amount of energy necessary to paint 1 m^2 is 37.2 joules (J). You determine the energy necessary to paint a bedroom of dimensions 4 m × 5 m × 2.4 m. The area of the walls is:

$$A = 2 \times 4m \times 2.4m + 2 \times 5m \times 2.4m = 42.3m^2$$

The required painting energy is:

$$E_{paint} = \frac{37.2J}{1m^2} \times 42.3m^2 = 1{,}573.6J$$

Now, according to the layout of the bedroom, you calculate the expenditure of energy to drag the furniture just to the door of the room:

$$\mathrm{E_{move}} = g\mu\left(\mathrm{m_{bed}d_{bed}} + \mathrm{m_{dresser}d_{dresser}} + \mathrm{m_{nightstand}d_{nightstand}} + \mathrm{m_{lamp}d_{lamp}}\right)$$

$$\mathrm{E_{move}} = 9.8\frac{\mathrm{m}}{\mathrm{s}^2} \times 0.6(47\mathrm{kg} \times 3.2\mathrm{m} + 25\mathrm{kg} \times 4.0\mathrm{m} + 6\mathrm{kg} \times 6.0\mathrm{m} + 3\mathrm{kg} \times 4.8\mathrm{m}) = 1{,}768.7\mathrm{J}$$

No need to calculate further; it is clear that the energy required to move furniture exceeds the energy it would take to paint. This energy can be used in much more useful ways, such as building a man cave (see Build a Man Cave).

h_{room}
$h_{ceiling}$
d_{lamp}
$d_{dresser}$
d_{bed}
$d_{nightstand}$

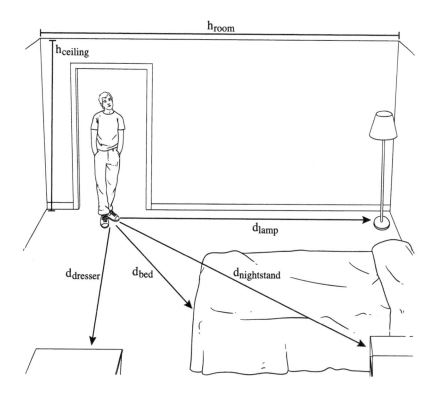

Fig. 4.b Get Out of Painting the Bedroom

4.c CLEAN THE HOUSE IN LESS THAN 10 MINUTES

You are leaving in 10 minutes for a date with the chick you met backstage (see Sneak

Backstage). Afterwards, you want to invite her to hang out at your place so you can put some

more man moves on her. Looking around the pad, you realize how nasty it is. Pizza boxes, boxer

shorts, clothes from who knows when, and beer cans all over the place. She'll never want to

hang out in these conditions. Hell, you don't even know where your couch is anymore—it's just

a pile of clothes on which you lounge. You determine you must clean. Calculate the time it will

take to put everything in its place. Assume the following variables and values:

Encumbered movement speed, s_e = 1 meter/second

Distance to dumpster, d_d = 53.1 meters

Distance to clothes drawer, d_c = 8.3 meters

Distance to recycle bin, d_r = 42 meters

Sifting time, t_s = 438 seconds

Number of dumpster trips, n_d = 5

Number of trips to clothes drawer, n_c = 4

Number of recylcing trips, n_r = 7

Total cleaning time for plan A is:

$$t_T = t_s + n_d \frac{d_d}{s_e} + n_r \frac{d_r}{s_e} + n_c \frac{d_c}{s_e} = 438s + 5\frac{53.1m}{1\frac{m}{s}} + 7\frac{42m}{1\frac{m}{s}} + 4\frac{8.3m}{1\frac{m}{s}} = 1{,}030.7s$$

Obviously, 10 minutes = 600 seconds. You don't have enough time. On to plan B.

Encumbered movement speed, s_e = 1 meter/second

Distance to closet, $d_{stuffit}$ = 10 meters

Number of trips to closet, $n_{stuffit} = n_d + n_c + n_r$

Total cleaning time for plan B is:

$$t_B = n_{stuffit} \frac{d_{stuffit}}{s_e} = \left(n_d + n_r + n_c\right) \frac{d_{stuffit}}{s_e} = 16 \frac{10m}{1\frac{m}{s}} = 160s$$

Your calculations show that stuffing everything in your closet is the correct option. With the time you have left over, you can sit on your new couch.

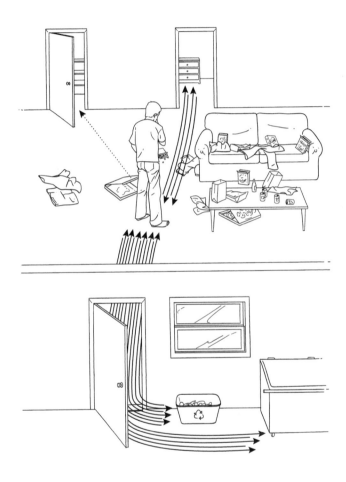

Fig. 4.c Clean the House in Less than 10 Minutes

4.d STEAL THE NEIGHBOR'S CABLE

It's almost like taking candy from a baby, only the candy is just hanging there on the side of the house and the baby is out of town. To access the cable lines, you need to climb a tree to reach the cable. You calculate the forces you will need to balance yourself while reaching for the cable. Equilibrate forces in the y-direction:

$$mg - f_{arm} \cos \theta_{arm} - f_{leg} \cos \theta_{leg} = 0$$

Equilibrate forces in the x-direction and solve for f_{leg}:

$$f_{arm} \sin \theta_{arm} - f_{leg} \sin \theta_{leg} = 0$$

$$f_{leg} = \frac{f_{arm} \sin \theta_{arm}}{\sin \theta_{leg}}$$

Plug in and solve for f_{arm} in the first equation, taking $\vartheta_{arm} = 90°$, $\vartheta_{leg} = 30°$, and $m = 73$ kg.

$$mg - f_{arm} \cos \theta_{arm} - \frac{f_{arm} \sin \theta_{arm}}{\sin \theta_{leg}} \cos \theta_{leg} = 0$$

$$f_{arm} = \frac{mg}{\cos \theta_{arm} + \frac{\sin \theta_{arm}}{\sin \theta_{leg}} \cos \theta_{leg}} = \frac{73 kg \times 9.8 \frac{m}{s^2}}{\cos 90° + \frac{\sin 90°}{\sin 30°} \cos 30°} = 413 N$$

Solve for f_{leg}:

$$f_{leg} = \frac{f_{arm} \sin \theta_{arm}}{\sin \theta_{leg}} = 413 N \frac{\sin 90°}{\sin 30°} = 826 N$$

With these forces, you can make the grab and rewire.

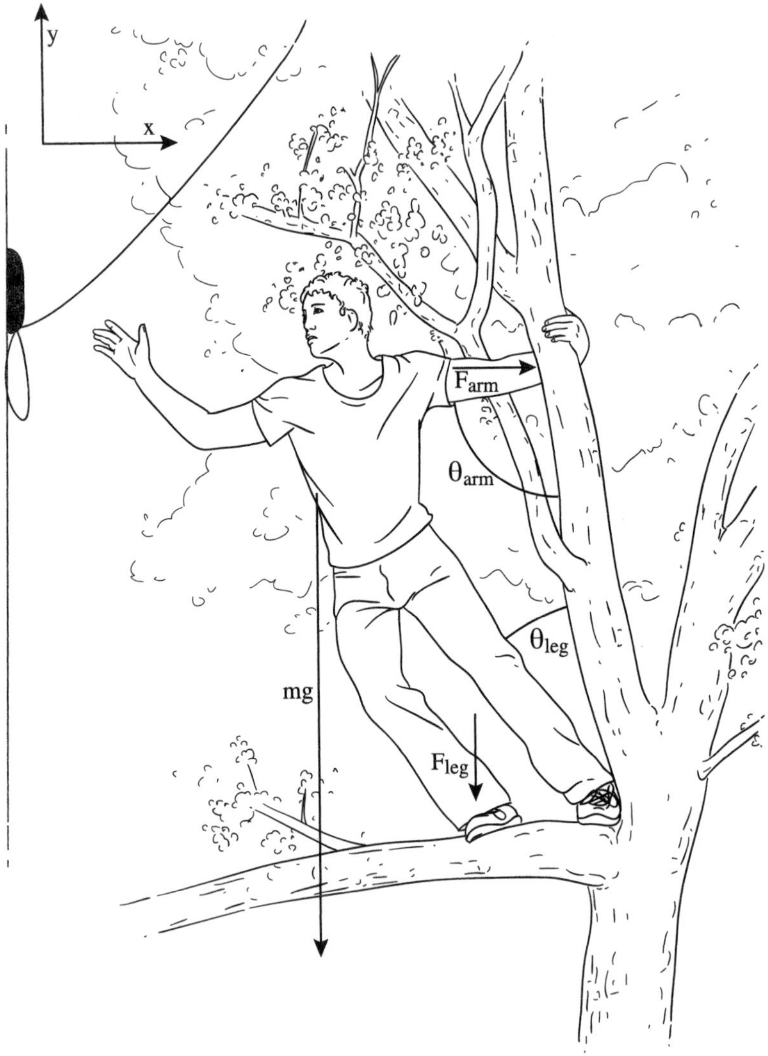
y
x
F_{arm}
θ_{arm}
θ_{leg}
mg
F_{leg}

Fig. 4.d Steal the Neighbor's Cable

4.e BUILD A MAN CAVE

Figure out the energy to create a man cave. The energy values to perform the work for certain man cave essentials have been determined by the Center for Man Caves and Their Usefulness. A representative table of these values follows.

ACTIVITY	ENERGY EXPENDED
Finish walls	34 J/m^2
Paint walls	32.7 J/m^2
Electrical wiring	26.2 J/m
Hang TV (27 kg)	264.6 J/m
Lay shag carpet	19.8 J/m^2
Install wet bar	400 J/m

Figure 4.5: Components of a Damn-Good Man Cave

For a man cave of dimensions 4 meters × 5 meters × 2.4 meters, you calculate the energy required. You decide to hang the TV centered at 1.8 meters and to install the wet bar along the 4-meter wall. The length of wiring you estimate that you will need is 25 meters. For these values:

$$E_{cave} = 34\frac{J}{m^2} \times 43.2m^2 + 32.7\frac{J}{m^2} \times 43.2m^2 + 26.2\frac{J}{m} \times 25m$$
$$+ 264.6\frac{J}{m} \times 1.8m + 19.8\frac{J}{m^2} \times 20m^2 + 400\frac{J}{m} \times 4m$$
$$E_{cave} = 6,008.72J$$

equation put forth by the Center for Man Caves and Their Usefulness to calculate the enjoyment number, M_{joy}, is:

$$M_{joy} = \frac{E_{cave}}{n} - 10h_w$$

where n is the number of days in a week and h_w is the height of the woman in your life who may not appreciate a man cave. If M_{joy} is determined to be a non-negative value, then you should move forward with the man cave project. Since every guy deserves a damn-good man cave, let's make h_w = 50 meters (which is over 150 feet—making it a man cave even Bruce Wayne would envy). Then:

$$M_{joy} = \frac{6,008.72J}{7} - 10 \times 50m = 358.72$$

Granted, your cave probably isn't this size. (A guy can dream, can't he?) Plug in your actual den dimensions to decide whether or not a Mecca of Manliness can actually make it in your house.

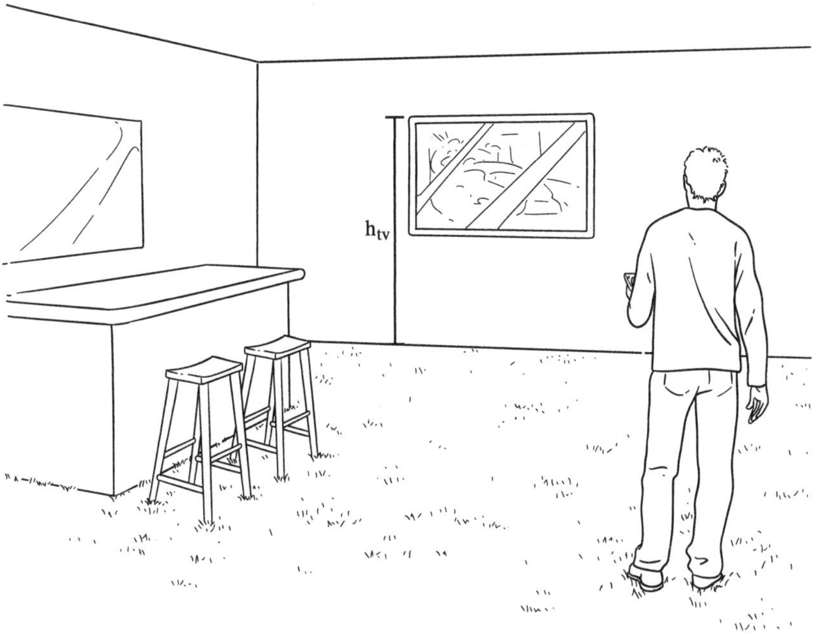
h_{tv}

Fig. 4.e Build a Man Cave

4.f CATCH A MOUSE

Forget those inhumane "humane" contraptions. Time to design your own trap—straight-up *Mouse Trap*-style. First, design a turntable with a pushbutton on/off switch located at the center. This is where the cheese will go. When the mouse removes the cheese from the switch, the table will start to rotate. The force necessary to depress the switch must be less than the weight of the cheese, $m_c = 0.01$ kilogram:

$$F_{switch} < m_{cheese}g = 0.01kg \times 9.8\frac{m}{s^2} = 0.98N$$

As the turntable rotates, the mouse will experience a centripetal force:

$$F_{cent} = m_{mouse}\frac{v^2}{r}$$

This force will continue to increase as the speed of rotation increases. When it equals the force of friction between the mouse and the surface of the table, the mouse will begin to slide farther and farther away from the center. Find the speed at which the table must rotate for the mouse to slide, letting $r = 0.03$ meter and $\mu = 0.4$.

$$m_{mouse}\frac{v^2}{r} = m_{mouse}g\mu$$
$$v = \sqrt{g\mu r} = \sqrt{9.8\frac{m}{s^2} \times 0.4 \times 0.03m} = 0.12\frac{m}{s}$$

At this point, the mouse is becoming disoriented and very dizzy. The mouse slides off the turntable into a funnel, which you have constructed out of chicken wire. The bottom of the funnel is tightly connected to a plastic ring. The mouth of a small drawstring sack fits just over the ring, and the end of the drawstring is tied to the chicken wire funnel. The mouse tumbles down the funnel and into the sack, which causes the sack to drop away from the end of the funnel and synches the drawstring sack to a close. The mouse is now caught, packaged, and ready for delivery.

g
F_{switch}
r
F_{cent}

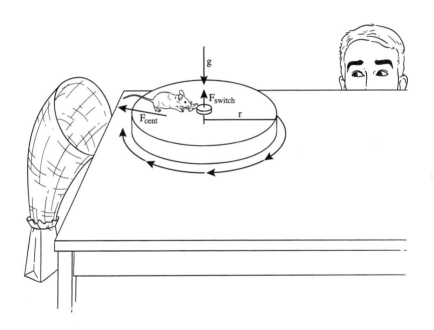

Fig. 4.f Catch a Mouse

4.g WALK THE DOG

Puppies are chick magnets. Determine the speed at which to walk one to attract the most women. Assume that the angular rate at which women can comfortably rotate their heads and make a decision to approach the puppy is 0.69 rad/s, if you are about 1.5 meters from the woman, then this corresponds to a linear velocity of:

$$v = \omega r = 0.69 \frac{rad}{s} \times 1.5m = 1.03 \frac{m}{s}$$

Obviously, this equation says that the closer she is to you, the slower you must walk to achieve the full effect. The puppy will have a mind of its own and may not be walking in the direction that is most effective. You must train it early to approach the cute chicks as closely as possible. Thus, you can enjoy a leisurely walk and reap the full benefits.

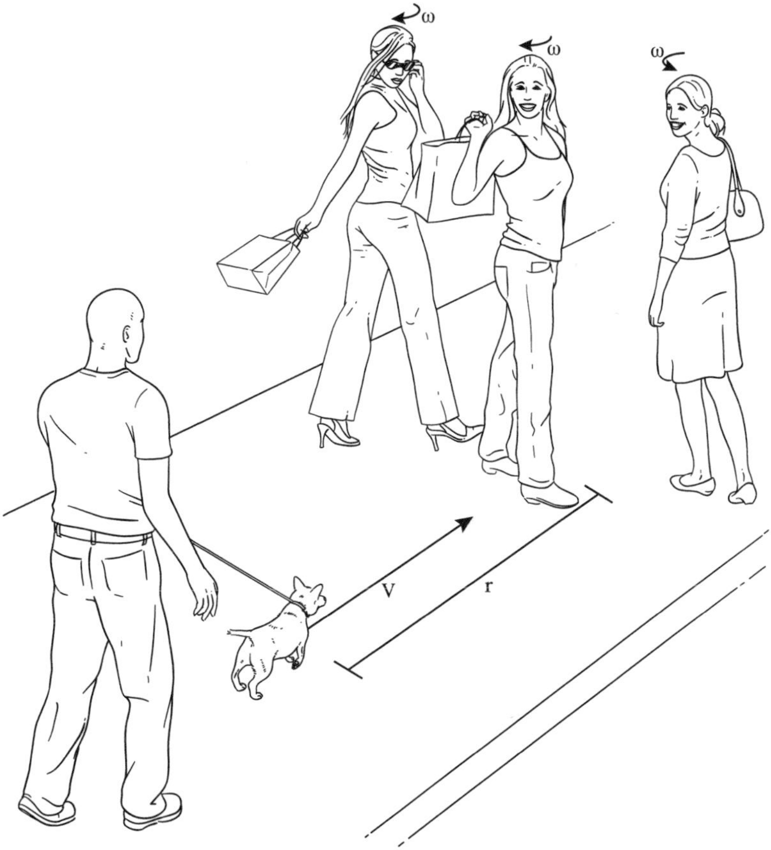
ω
ω
ω
V
r

Fig. 4.g Walk the Dog

4.h PEE WITH THE SEAT DOWN

No need to lift, just determine the correct angle of attack for the stream. The target should be the steepest portion of the toilet bowl. This gives the smallest splash. Assume the following parameters:

v_p: the initial speed of flow = 0.5 meter/second

h_t: target height in toilet = 0.13 meter

h_p: launching height = 1.7 meters

d_t: distance from target = 1.56 meters

The equation of motion in terms of the angle is:

$$\frac{gd_t^2}{2v_p^2}\tan^2\theta + d_t\tan\theta + h_t - h_p + \frac{gd_t^2}{2v_p^2} = 0$$

Solve this equation for ϑ:

$$\theta = \tan^{-1}\left(\frac{-d_t \pm \sqrt{d_t^2 - \frac{2gd_t^2}{v_p^2}\left(h_t - h_p + \frac{gd_t^2}{2v_p^2}\right)}}{\frac{ad_t^2}{v_p^2}}\right)$$

$$= \tan^{-1}\left(\frac{-1.57\text{m} \pm \sqrt{(1.56\text{m})^2 - \frac{2\times 9.8\frac{\text{m}}{\text{s}^2}\times(1.56\text{m})^2}{\left(0.5\frac{\text{m}}{\text{s}}\right)^2}\left(0.13\text{m} - 1.7\text{m} + \frac{9.8\frac{\text{m}}{\text{s}^2}\times(1.56\text{m})^2}{2\times\left(0.5\frac{\text{m}}{\text{s}}\right)^2}\right)}}{\frac{9.8\frac{\text{m}}{\text{s}^2}\times(1.56\text{m})^2}{\left(0.5\frac{\text{m}}{\text{s}}\right)^2}}\right)$$

$$= \tan^{-1}\left(\frac{-1.57\text{m} \pm 1.56\text{m}}{30.57\text{m}}\right)$$

This gives values of $\theta = 0.02°$ below the horizontal or $\theta = 5.8°$ above the horizontal. Your choice.

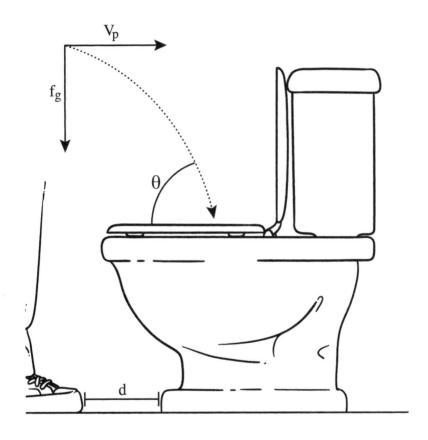

Fig. 4.h Pee with the Seat Down

4.i CRAM EVERY DIRTY DISH
INTO THE DISHWASHER

Get the most out of every dishwashing load, especially if you are not the one to have to unload

it. Calculate how much force you can apply to close the door without destroying the

Tupperware®. Assume an average Tupperware failure force of f_f = 196 newtons (N). Determine

the force of the door on a piece of Tupperware. Use the following variables to determine

pertinent torques:

d: distance from hinge where you apply closing force = 0.7 meter

r: distance of Tupperware from hinge of door = 0.3 meter

F_{push}: maximum force with which you can push the door closed (what you are seeking)

F_{cram}: maximum force the door can exert on Tupperware = 196 newtons (N)

ϑ_{push}: angle at which F_{push} is applied = 87°

The torque from F_{push} is:

$$\tau_{push} = dF_{push} \sin \theta_{push}$$

And from F_{cram} is:

$$\tau_{cram} = rF_{cram}$$

Determine the maximum force with which you can push the dishwasher door closed.

$$\tau_{cram} = \tau_{push}$$
$$rF_{cram} = dF_{push} \sin \theta_{push}$$
$$F_{push} = \frac{rF_{cram}}{d \sin \theta_{push}} = \frac{0.3m \times 196N}{0.7m \times \sin 87°} = 84.1N$$

With this force and angle of push, you can be sure to maximize the packing and minimize the

breaking.

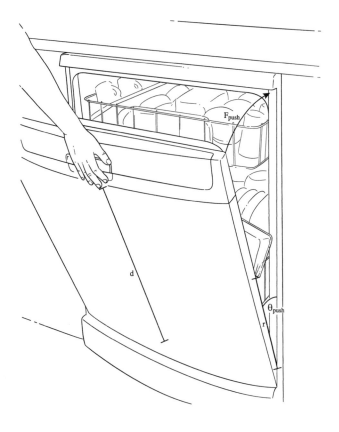

Fig. 4.i Cram Every Dirty Dish into the Dishwasher

4.j MOVE A COUCH THROUGH A DOORWAY

Calculate the energy required to navigate a couch through a doorway. You have the following variables:

m_c: mass of the couch = 53 kilograms

l_c: length of couch = 2.4 meters

μ: coefficient of kinetic friction between couch and floor = 0.4

r: radial distance of center of mass of couch from door frame during rotation = 0.7 meter

ϑ: angle through which couch must be rotated at doorway = 110°

Energy to stand couch on end:

$$E_1 = m_c g \frac{l_c}{2} = 53kg \times 9.8 \frac{m}{s^2} \times \frac{2.4m}{2} = 623J$$

Energy required to rotate the couch about the door frame:

$$E_2 = N\mu r\theta = m_c g\mu r\theta = 53kg \times 9.8\frac{m}{s^2} \times 0.4 \times 0.7m \times 110° \times \frac{\pi}{180°} = 279J$$

Adding these energies up yields:

$$E_T = E_1 + E_2 = 623J + 279J = 902J$$

This is the total energy that is required for the move. Of course, who cares about the energy?

The real concern is whether there is enough beer in the cooler for *after* the move.

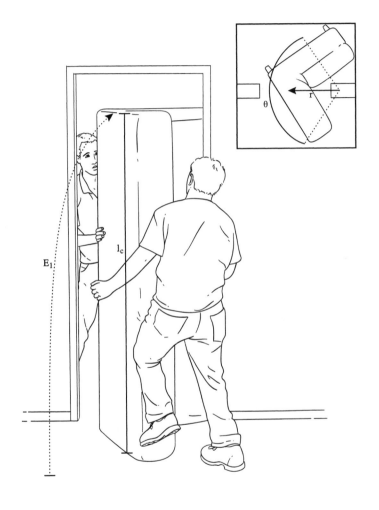

Fig. 4.j Move a Couch through a Doorway

4.k CHANGE A HIGH LIGHT BULB
WITHOUT A LADDER

Ladder schmadder. You can change the light bulb with a carefully choreographed combination of jumping and turning. Assume that it takes about five complete turns to unscrew the bulb. With each jump, you can turn the bulb about 1/5 of a turn. Calculate the number of jumps required:

$$n = \frac{5\,turns}{\frac{1}{5}\,\frac{turns}{jump}} = 25\,jumps$$

Of course, this is only the number of jumps to remove the burned-out bulb. Double this for the replacement with a new bulb. Calculate the time it takes to do the change. For a jump height of 0.6 meter, the round-trip jump time is:

$$t = 2\sqrt{\frac{2h}{g}} = 2\sqrt{\frac{2 \times 0.6m}{9.8\frac{m}{s^2}}} = 0.7s$$

For 50 jumps, the total time is:

$$T = 50t = 50 \times 0.7s = 35s$$

How many ladders does it take to replace a light bulb? With physics—*none.*

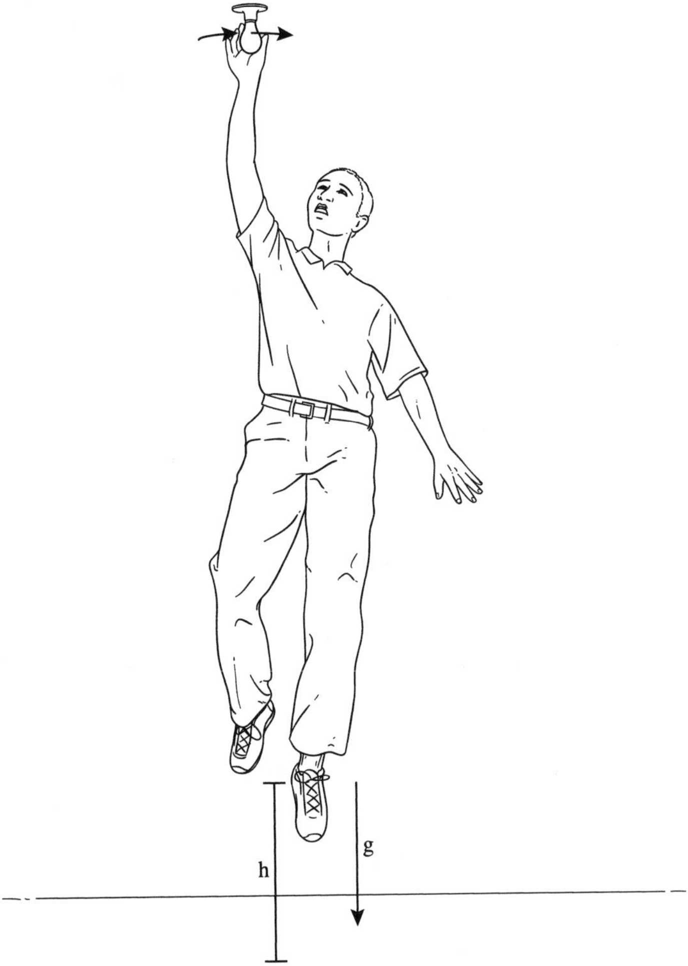
h
g

Fig. 4.k Change a High Light Bulb Without a Ladder

4.I MOW THE LAWN AS QUICKLY AS POSSIBLE

You don't want to waste the whole day out in the yard, so you determine the theoretical

shortest time for mowing. Assume the motor drives the blade at a full rotation in 0.25 second.

This gives the blade an angular speed of:

$$\omega = \frac{\Delta\theta}{\Delta t} = \frac{2\pi}{0.25s} = 25.1\frac{rad}{s}$$

For a blade of radius 0.3 meter, the outside of the blade is moving at a linear speed of:

$$v = \omega r = 25.1\frac{rad}{s} \times 0.3m = 7.5\frac{m}{s}$$

Assume that the lawn mower blade has to hit a blade of grass at a speed of 2 meters/second to

cut it. Then the fastest that you will be able to push the mower without missing a blade of grass

is:

$$v_m = 7.5\frac{m}{s} - 2\frac{m}{s} = 5.5\frac{m}{s}$$

For a yard of dimensions 35 meters × 29 meters, the time it takes to make a pass for each

dimension is:

$$t_{35} = \frac{35m}{5.5\frac{m}{s}} = 6.36s$$

$$t_{29} = \frac{29m}{5.5\frac{m}{s}} = 5.27s$$

For a cut width = 0.6 meter, the number of passes needed for each dimension is:

$$n_{29} = \frac{29m}{0.6m} = 48.3$$

$$n_{35} = \frac{35m}{0.6m} = 58.3$$

$$T_{35} = t_{35}n_{29} = 6.36s \times 48.3 = 307s$$
$$T_{29} = t_{29}n_{35} = 5.27s \times 58.3 = 307s$$

Theoretically, both ways will take the same amount of time, which is the fastest possible time for this job.

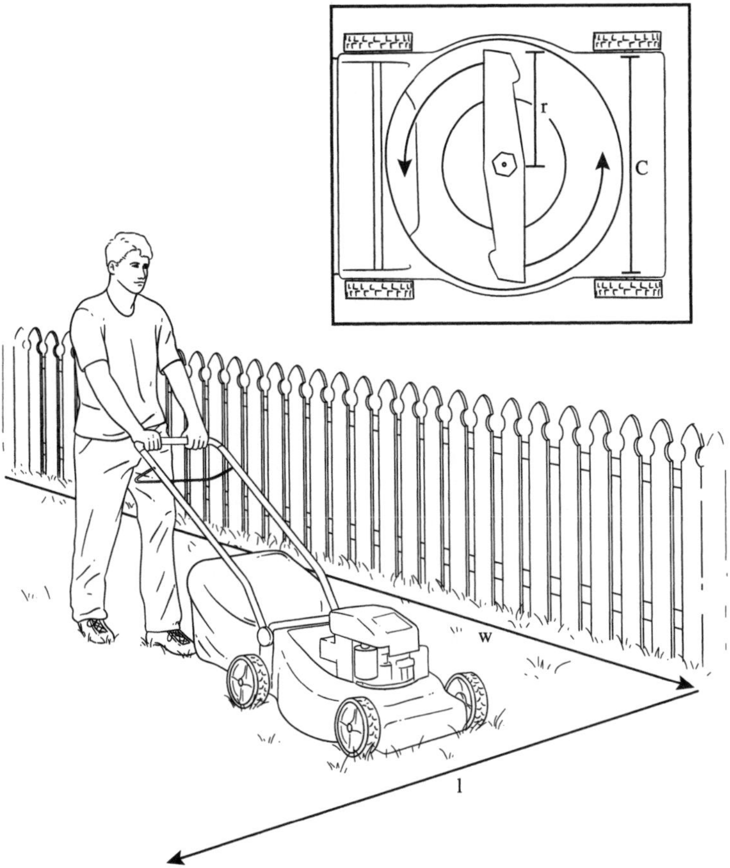
r
C
w
l

Fig. 4.1 Mow the Lawn as Quickly as Possible

LESSONS IN THIS CHAPTER

WOMEN

5.a BE THE WINGMAN:
EVASIVE MANEUVER #1

You know the rules: finders keepers. He saw her first. Playing the wingman involves both skill

and precision. Since your bud isn't gonna have any clue what he is doing, it is up to you.

Calculate evasive maneuvers if the girl starts to talk to you.

You need to move from a shoulder-to-shoulder position to one that gives your bud the spotlight.

Calculate the new angle and distance relative to your bud and his target.

d_g: distance from buddy to girl = 0.5 meter

d_{bi}: initial distance from you to buddy = 1.0 meter

d_s: distance you move back = 0.5 meter

d_{bf}: final distance from you to buddy

ϑ_i: initial angle from girl to you = 84°

ϑ_f: final angle from girl to you =

$$d_{bf} = \sqrt{d_s^2 + d_{bi}^2} = \sqrt{(0.5m)^2 + (1.0m)^2} = 1.12m$$

$$\theta_f = \tan^{-1}\frac{d_g + d_s}{d_{bi}} = \tan^{-1}\frac{0.5m + 0.5m}{1.0m} = 45°$$

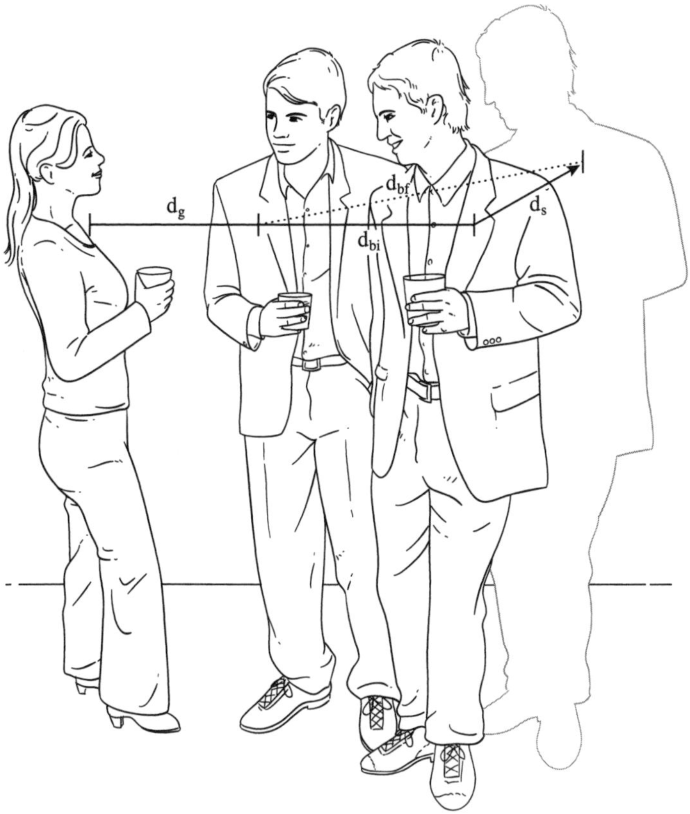
d_g
d_{bf}
d_{bi}
d_s

Fig. 5.a Be the Wingman: Evasive Maneuver #1

5.b BE THE WINGMAN:
EVASIVE MANEUVER #2

The girl looks as if she might start talking to you. You need to make it difficult for her. Duck and cover by fake tying your shoelaces. Determine the minimum time it will take for you to drop into a crouch position.

h_i: height of your center of mass when standing = 1.7 meters

h_f: height of your center of mass when tying shoe = 0.6 meter

t: time it takes to drop:

$$t = \sqrt{\frac{2(h_i - h_f)}{g}} = \sqrt{\frac{2(1.7m - 0.6)}{9.8\frac{m}{s}}} = 0.47s$$

Since it will take her .5s to figure out what to say to you, you have safely disappeared before you unwittingly poach your buddy's prospects.

Then there's always Evasive Maneuver #3: Take a Bathroom Break. This is your last-ditch effort to focus all attention on your buddy. Make sure to cover your butt as you walk away, because you know she will be checking it out.

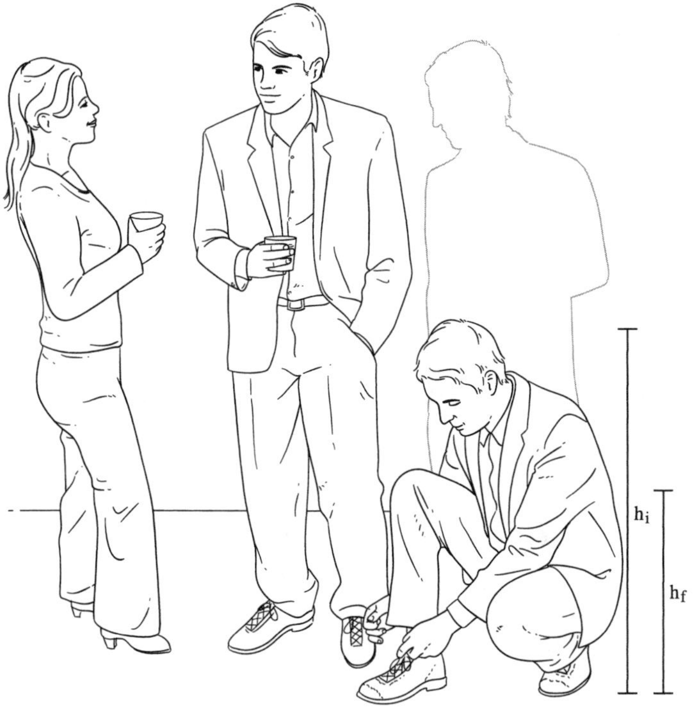
h_i
h_f

Fig. 5.b Be the Wingman: Evasive Maneuver #2

5.c PICK UP THE HOTTIE AT THE BAR

There she sits across the bar. Fleeting eye contact has been made. It's time to calculate an

intercept trajectory with the appropriate timing. You see that the speed of rotation of her head

is about ω_h and her average rotational deviation is ϑ. Plan to initiate your intercept when she is

beginning her angular sweep away from you. Chances are, she is into that weird vampire crap,

so it will work in your favor if all of a sudden you just appear by her side. The variables are:

d: distance you must travel = 3.4 meters

ω_h: angular velocity of her head = 30 rad/s

ϑ: angle of deviation of her head = $\pi/2$

Calculate the time you have to move and the speed you have to do it with:

$$t = \frac{2\theta}{\omega_h} = \frac{2 \times \frac{\pi}{2}}{30\frac{rad}{s}} = 6s$$

$$v = \frac{3.4m}{6s} = 0.57\frac{m}{s}$$

Moving at this rate, you will appear by her side when she is looking straight ahead. Move in

beside her and give her the schpeel. Wrap it up by inviting her out to the carnival.

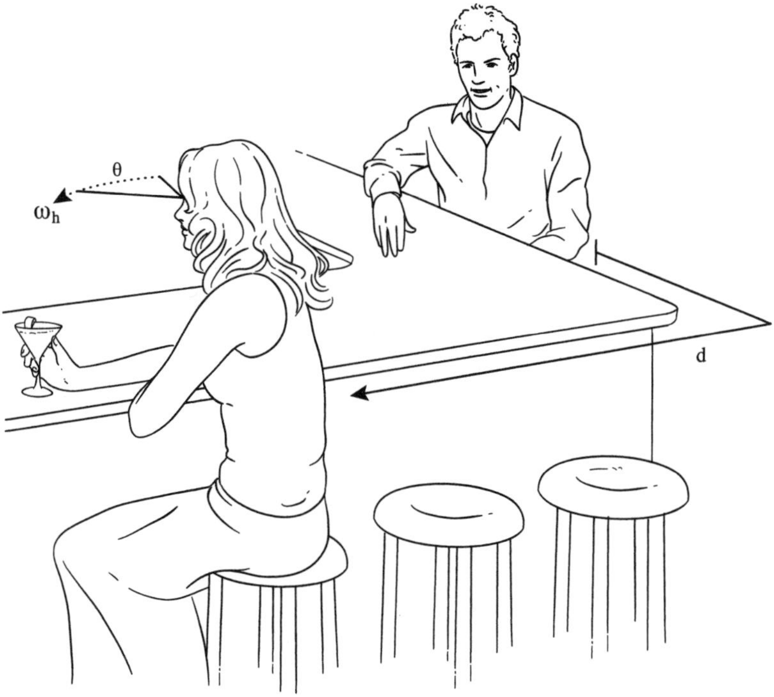
θ
ω_h
d

Fig. 5.c Pick Up the Hottie at the Bar

5.d WIN HER A TEDDY BEAR AT THE CARNIVAL

The games are rigged, but your lady wants a prize. You determine the extra momentum

required to beat the strongman game. A little recon is in order. Watching the lug ahead of you,

you note the following values:

s_{ham}: speed of the hammer when it hits the lever = 13 meters/second

m_{plug}: mass of plug = 0.25 kilogram

h_t: height of bell = 9.7 meters

h_m: height the plug reaches with s_{ham} = 7.8 meters

Determine the energy loss in this hokey game by using the height that the plug should have

reached, h_T.

$$m_{plug} g h_T = \frac{1}{2} m_{plug} s_{ham}^2$$

$$h_T = \frac{s_{ham}^2}{2g}$$

$$\Delta E = m_{plug} g \frac{s_{ham}^2}{2g} - m_{plug} g h_m = 0.25kg \times \frac{\left(13\frac{m}{s}\right)^2}{2} - 0.25kg \times 9.8\frac{m}{s^2} \times 7.8m = 2J$$

Calculate the extra energy required to hit the bell with s_{ham}:

$$E_x = m_{plug} g h_t - m_{plug} g h_m = 0.25kg \times 9.8\frac{m}{s^2} \times 9.7m - 0.25kg \times 9.8\frac{m}{s^2} \times 7.8m = 4.7J$$

You know your swing speed is 12.2 meters/second. Calculate how much more swing energy you

need to outperform the other guy:

$$E_s = \frac{1}{2} m_{plug} s_{ham}^2 - \frac{1}{2} m_{plug} s_{you}^2 = \frac{1}{2} \times 0.25kg \times \left(\left(13\frac{m}{s}\right)^2 - \left(12.2\frac{m}{s}\right)^2\right) = 2.5J$$

You need to generate 6.7 J more energy than the last guy. Determine how high your center of mass needs to move to create this energy:

$$h_{com} = \frac{\Delta E + E_x + E_s}{m_{you}g} = \frac{9.2J}{62kg \times 9.8\frac{m}{s^2}} = 0.015m$$

So to beat the game, you lift your body up 0.015 meter at the height of the swing and show your baby who's the man.

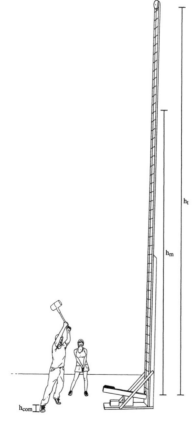

Fig. 5.d Win Her a Teddy Bear at the Carnival

5.e DIP HER (WITHOUT DROPPING HER)

A dip is a romantic way to end a dance, but be sure to calculate the forces required to do it in balance. Assume that the dipee knows that she needs to keep firm while being dipped. If she doesn't, no guarantees here. You may end up on top of her, both of you on the floor. You might not think that would be so bad either, but let's not digress.

Use Newton's Second Law to find the force you need to apply:

$$F_m d_m \sin\theta_M = F_h d_h \sin\theta_h$$
$$F_m = \frac{F_h d_h \sin\theta_h}{d_m \sin\theta_M} = \frac{m_{girl} g d_h \sin\theta_h}{2 d_m \sin\theta_M}$$

For a girl of mass 61.2 kilograms, ϑ_h = 33°, and ϑ_M = 99°,

$$F_m = \frac{m_{girl} g d_h \sin\theta_h}{2 d_m \sin\theta_M} = \frac{61.2kg \times 9.8\frac{m}{s^2} \times 1.53m \times \sin 33°}{2 \times 1.29m \times \sin 99°} = 196N$$

With 196N of force and some serious physics swagger, you'll give her the dip of her life. And with a little chemistry, these won't be the only moves you two make tonight.

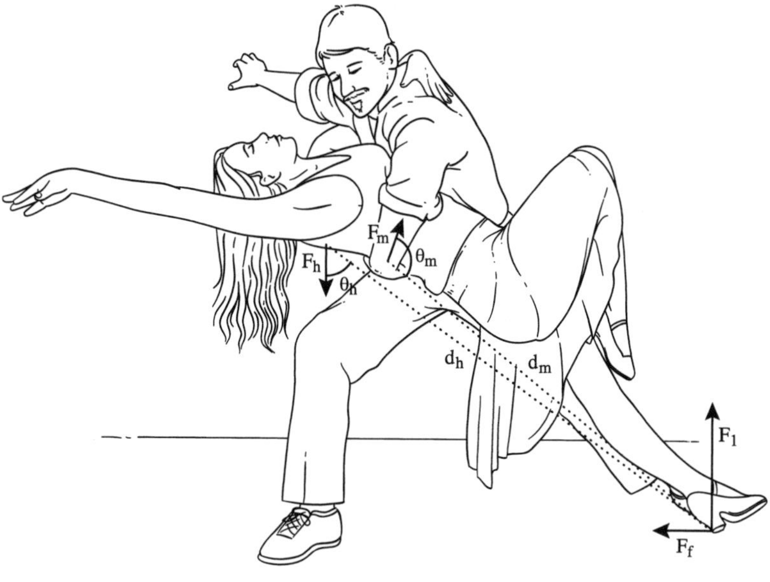
F_m
θ_m
F_h
θ_h
d_h
d_m
F_l
F_f

Fig. 5.e Dip Her (Without Dropping Her)

5.f ESCAPE A SPOONING

There are a time and a place for spooning and cuddling. Usually the time is no time, and the place is nowhere. If you are caught in one, you need to be able to escape. Knowing what you know about friction, you determine the appropriate way to escape. Assuming her arm is over yours, determine the force of static friction between your arm and hers:

$$f_s = N\mu = m_{arm}g\mu = 2.6kg \times 9.8\frac{m}{s^2} \times 0.4 = 10.4N$$

You know that the force of kinetic friction is less than that of static friction, so you want to get your arm moving. The probability of her waking is related to the time you have been in the spooning position, T_{spoon}, to the normalized body contact length, $L_N = L/0.001$ meter; and to the time it takes to overcome f_s, Δt. Calculate it as

$$P_{sleep} = \frac{L_N \Delta t}{T_{spoon}}$$

Unfortunately, you realize that time spent spooning will greatly assist in your escaping. However, the tradeoff is how quickly you can overcome f_s. To minimize it, determine how long it takes your muscles to reach the necessary force. It takes you about 0.1 second to move your arm from 0 meter/second to 4 meters/second. Take the mass of your arm to be 3 kilograms. So:

$$\frac{\Delta f}{\Delta t} = m\frac{\Delta a}{\Delta t} = m\frac{\Delta v}{(\Delta t)^2} = 3kg\frac{4\frac{m}{s}}{(0.2s)^2} = 100\frac{N}{s}$$

The time to overcome the force of static friction is:

$$\Delta t = \frac{\Delta f}{1200\frac{N}{s}} = \frac{10.4N}{100\frac{N}{s}} = 0.104s$$

Find the necessary spooning time for P_{sleep} = 0.51 and L = 3.2 meters:

$$T_{spoon} = \frac{L_N \Delta t}{P_{sleep}} = \frac{\dfrac{3.2m}{0.001m} \times 0.104s}{0.49} = 679s$$

Of course, if you were silly enough to get your fingers intertwined with hers, then God help ya

and good luck!

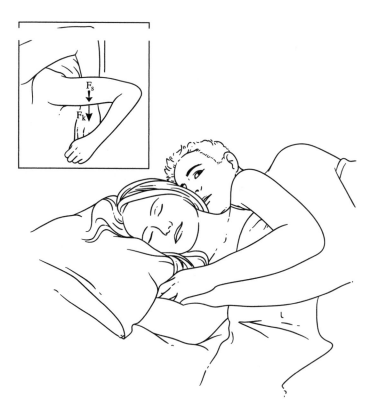

Fig. 5.f Escape a Spooning

5.g EVAC AFTER A ONE-NIGHT STAND

Assuming that you have successfully escaped the spooning (see Escape a Spooning), now it is time to evacuate. Her apartment, that is. Speed and stealth are the primary concerns. Dressing speed is directly proportional to the energy you exert doing it:

$$E = \frac{1}{2}mv^2$$

Worst-case scenario, you can pull on your pants and scram out the door with your other accoutrements in tow. To avoid excessive creaking of the floors, you make your energy of pulling on your pants less than the energy required to create a creak. Calculate the creaking energy, using the force that the floor joints exert on each other, F = 30J, and the distance of joint movements against each other, d = 0.001 meter.

$$E_{creak} = Fd = 30J \times 0.001m = 0.03J$$

Calculate the speed with which you may pull on your pants, neglecting leg/pants friction (not because you shave your legs, or anything like that, but just because):

$$v = \sqrt{\frac{2E_{creak}}{m_{pants}}} = \sqrt{\frac{2 \times 0.03J}{0.5kg}} = 0.35\frac{m}{s}$$

And make a run!

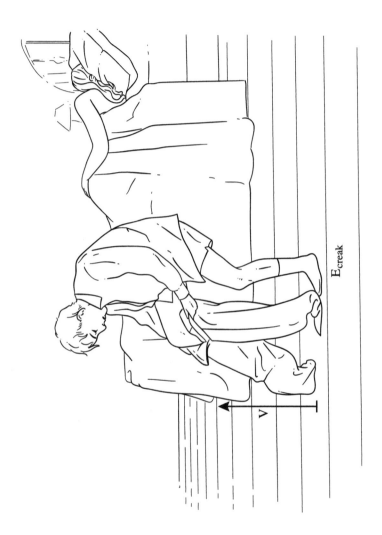

Fig. 5.g Evac after a One-Night Stand

E_{creak}

v

5.h HIT ON TWO WOMEN AT ONCE

Hitting on one woman is good; hitting on two is even better. You determine the appropriate time and frequency characteristics for this activity. Assume that the women are separated by an angle of $\psi = 0.69$ rad. The angular frequency of titillating woman A, rotating your head to woman B, exciting her, and then returning to the other is:

$$\omega = \frac{2\psi}{t_{comp}}$$

Determine t_{comp} such that you don't get yourself dizzy. It is calculated as:

$$t_{comp} = G_e t E_m N_{aked}$$

Where:

G_e: the effective "googly eyes" number. It is how much they are ogling you. Scale of 1 to 10.

t: the average time your eye remains on either woman as you are turning to the other one

E_m: the manliness that you are emitting (depends on clothing, cologne, hair care, and smile; scale of 1 to 10)

N_{aked}: the running total of pickup lines you have used so far, divided by 20

Assume $G_e = 6$, $t = 0.7$s, $E_m = 5$, and $N_{aked} = 3$. Then:

$$\omega = \frac{2\psi}{t_{comp}} = \frac{2\psi}{G_e t E_m N_{aked}} = \frac{2 \times 0.69 rad}{6 \times 0.7s \times 5 \times \dfrac{3}{20}} = 0.3 \frac{rad}{s}$$

With this rate of head rotation, you will be able not only to hit on *these* chicks but also to scan the room for more action while you are doing it.

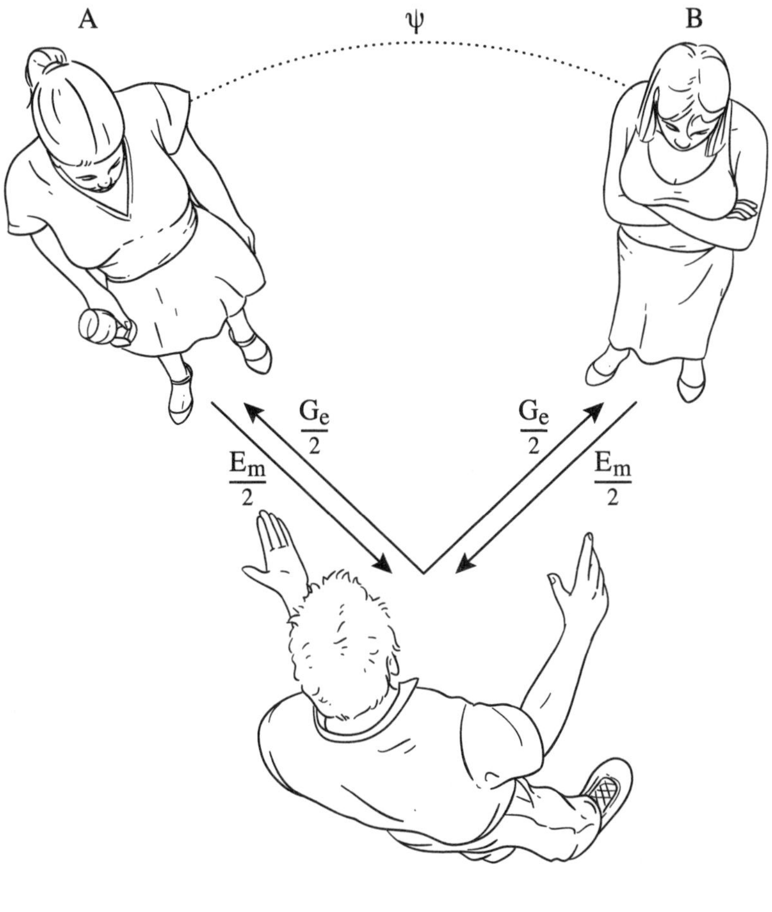
A
ψ
B
$\frac{G_e}{2}$
$\frac{G_e}{2}$
$\frac{E_m}{2}$
$\frac{E_m}{2}$

Fig. 5.h Hit on Two Women at Once

5.i SEPARATE A GIRL FROM A COCKBLOCKER

Just a bit of annoyance is all. You determine the necessary force required to gracefully box her

friend out while still maintaining the connection to the party of interest. Think basketball

rebound here. The shot is up, so you box out your opponent and get ready to score the

rebound. Assume that the blocker has a mass of m_{cb} = 58 kilograms, and she is moving with an

average speed of s_{cb} = 0.5 meter/second. Determine the contact force you must exert to keep

the blocker boxed by applying the formula:

$$F = \frac{m_{cb}\Delta s_{cb}}{\Delta t}$$

For an average contact time of Δt = 0.4 second and a complete change of direction of the

blocker:

$$F = \frac{m_{cb}\Delta s_{cb}}{\Delta t} = \frac{58kg \times 1.0\frac{m}{s}}{0.4s} = 145N$$

This force to maintain a blocker box will exert a torque on you. Assume the blocker contacts

your arm at a distance r = 0.6 meter from your shoulder and an angle θ = 107°. Then the torque

about the shoulder is:

$$\tau = Fr\sin\theta = 145N \times 0.6m \times \sin 107 = 83Nm$$

Counteract this torque with large shoulder and back muscles to make it look effortless. Be aware

that blockers sometimes jump to insert their pesky dialogue over your shoulder. No worries, just

maintain the box, since her jump will not cause you any extra exertion.

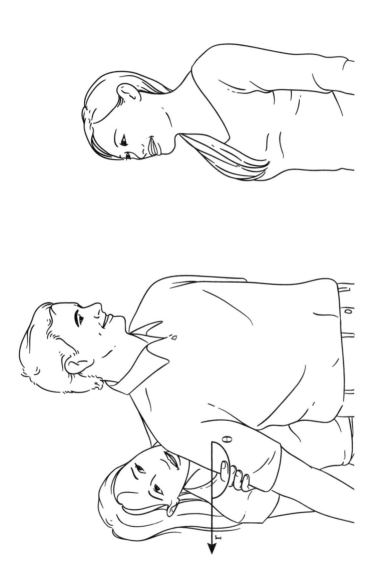

Fig. 5.i Separate a Girl from a Cockblocker

5.j TAKE HER UPSTAIRS

Question: Why prolong the inevitable? Answer: Because it might be fun. You calculate the energy required to carry her up the stairs for some lovin'. Assume there are 18 stairs with a height of 0.17 meter each and your lovemaking machine has a mass of 65 kilograms.

$$E = Fd = mgh = 65kg \times 9.8\frac{m}{s^2} \times 18 \times 0.17m = 1,949J$$

Now calculate the power required to mount the stairs. The stairs, man, the *stairs*.

$$P = \frac{E}{t}$$

Use two different values of t. Your fastest stair sprint speed is 0.93 meter/second. The distance of the sprint is 5.3 meters. For these values, the power is:

$$P_{sprint} = \frac{E}{t} = \frac{1,949J}{5.3m\bigg/3\frac{m}{s}} = 342W$$

Now assume you take your time, getting a little frisky on the way, so that $t = 60$ seconds:

$$P_{frisky} = \frac{E}{t} = \frac{1949J}{60s} = 32.5W$$

Deciding between the sprint and the frisk involves calculating the heat-of-the-moment factor:

$$H_m = h_{him} + h_{her} - \frac{P_{sprint}}{P_{frisk} + 1.7W}$$

h_{him}: hot-to-trot value for you on a scale of 1–10; h_{her}: hot-to-trot value for her on a scale of 1–10

For a representative calculation, take $h_{him} = 10$ and $h_{her} = 3$:

$$H_m = h_{him} + h_{her} - \frac{P_{sprint}}{P_{frisk} + 1.7W} = 10 + 3 - \frac{1,103W}{32.5W + 1.7W} = 3$$

For $H_m \le 11$, chose the frisky climb. By the time you are halfway up the stairs, you may have to start to sprint, regardless.

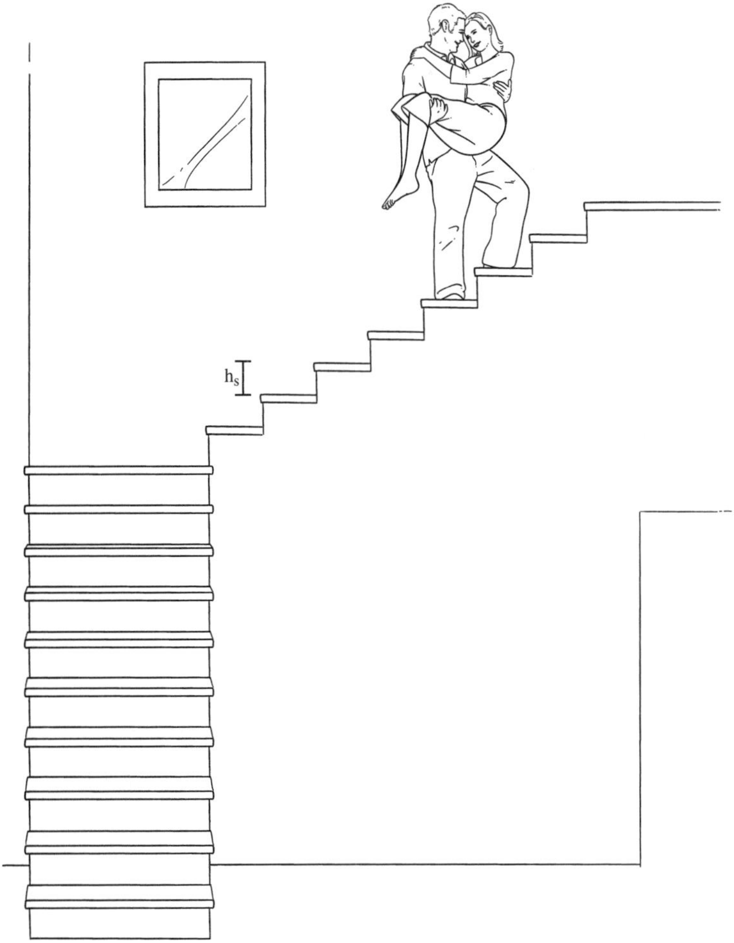
h_s

Fig. 5.j Take Her Upstairs

5.k SWITCH POSITIONS

Switching positions is a great way to create diversity. You determine the energy it will take to switch from you on top to her on top. Assume the following values:

m_m: your mass = 89 kilograms

m_h: her mass = 70.8 kilograms

h_h: height of her center of mass when she is on top = 0.32 meter

h_m: height of your center of mass when you are on top = 0.25 meter

$$E_{switch} = m_m gh_m + m_h gh_h = 90kg \times 9.8\frac{m}{s^2} \times 0.28m + 70.8kg \times 9.8\frac{m}{s^2} \times 0.32m = 469J$$

Just because you *can* switch positions, doesn't mean you necessarily *should*. Calculate the efficiency of the switch:

$$e_{switch} = \left(1 - \frac{E_{switch}}{E_{new}}\right) \times 100$$

E_{out} is the renewed energy you get from being in the new position. Determine it using:

$$E_{new} = 469J\left(p_m + p_h\right)$$

p_m and p_h are the added pleasure factors for you and for her, respectively, on a scale of 1 to 100. The efficiency is given as a percent, and the closer e_{switch} is to 100 percent, the better it is to make a move. For a sample calculation, assume that p_m = 100 and p_h = 100:

$$e_{switch} = \left(1 - \frac{E_{switch}}{E_{new}}\right) \times 100 = \left(1 - \frac{469J}{469J\left(100 + 100\right)}\right) \times 100 = 99.5\%$$

This is the absolute best efficiency you can get out of the repositioning. If you can attain this value, by all means, switch positions!

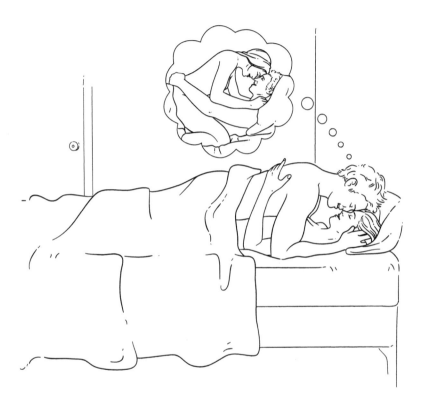

Fig. 5.k Switch Positions

5.I HAVE SEX IN A RISKY LOCATION

Exhibitionist? No need for calculations. You'll just let it all hang out anyway. However, if you

crave the risk but abhor the embarrassment (and possible jail time), it may be necessary to

utilize parallax to your advantage. Assume you are at the public park, behind a tree. A potential

voyeur is looking directly at it. Calculate how much room you have in which to maneuver behind

the tree and still stay out of eyesight. Take the following values:

d_t: diameter of tree = 0.66 meter

d_e: distance between voyeur's eyes = 0.007 meter

d_v: distance of voyeur from center of tree = 10 meters

d_p: distance of point source

Find d_p:

$$d_p = \frac{d_v}{\dfrac{d_t}{d_e} - 1} = \frac{10m}{\dfrac{0.66m}{.007m} - 1} = 0.11m$$

Find the angle ϑ:

$$\theta = \tan^{-1} \frac{d_e}{2d_p} = \tan^{-1} \frac{0.007m}{2 \times 0.11m} = 1.87°$$

If you are an additional 0.38 meter away from the center of the tree, determine how far outside

the diameter of the tree you can be:

$$d_{extra} = d_{invisible} - d_t = (d_p + d_v + 0.38m)\tan\theta - \frac{d_t}{2} = (0.11m + 10m + 0.38m)\tan 1.87° - \frac{0.66m}{2}$$
$$= 0.012m$$

That's an additional 1.2 centimeters. Keep it tight, man, keep it tight.

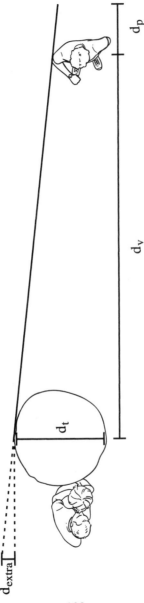

d_p

d_v

d_t

d_{extra}

Fig. 5.1 Have Sex in a Risky Location

5.m SURPRISE HER WITH A PROPOSAL

A carnival is the perfect setting for a surprise proposal. You already thoroughly impressed her by winning that teddy bear (see Win Her a Teddy Bear at the Carnival). Now you need to surprise her with the ring. Since your babe wants to ride the yo-yo swing ride, you calculate the correct trajectory with which to toss the ring box so that it will land on her lap. Waiting in line, you note that the angular speed of the swings is $\omega = 0.78$ rad/s and that the chairs are a distance $d = 2$ meters apart and at a radius of $r = 18$ meters. Calculate the velocity with which to toss the ring to counter the swing velocity:

$$v_x = \omega r = 0.78 \frac{rad}{s} \times 18m = 14 \frac{m}{s}$$

This is the horizontal velocity in the direction opposite to the motion of the swing. The time it will take her chair to travel a distance d, then, is:

$$t = \frac{d}{v_x} = \frac{2m}{14 \frac{m}{s}} = 0.14s$$

Determine the vertical velocity:

$$v_y = \frac{gt}{2} = \frac{9.8 \frac{m}{s^2} \times 0.14s}{2} = 0.7 \frac{m}{s}$$

The total velocity and angle are:

$$v = \sqrt{v_x^2 + v_y^2} = \sqrt{\left(14 \frac{m}{s}\right)^2 + \left(0.7 \frac{m}{s}\right)^2} = 14.02 \frac{m}{s}$$

$$\theta = \tan^{-1} \frac{0.7 \frac{m}{s}}{14 \frac{m}{s}} = 2.86°$$

These values guarantee that the ring will land on her lap. When it does, and she recovers from her surprise and opens the box, you shout back, "Will you marry me?" How could she resist?

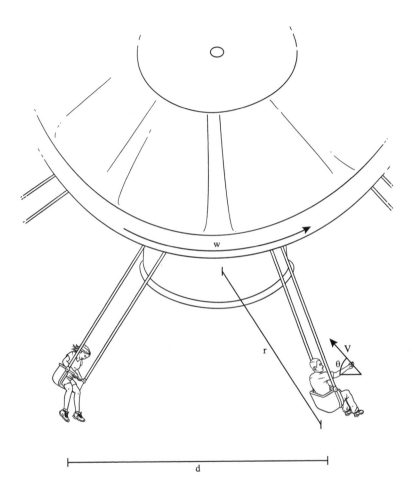

Fig. 5.m Surprise Her with a Proposal

LESSONS IN THIS CHAPTER

SLEEP

6.a FIND THE PERFECT NAPPING POSITION

The perfect couch-napping position is defined by comfort. You determine the proper support for your body parts while lying on your back. For your head, you use a pillow of height 0.006 meter when compacted. This gives a neck angle of:

$$\eta = \tan^{-1}\frac{h_{head}}{l_{neck}} = \tan^{-1}\frac{0.006m}{0.17m} = 2.02°$$

You drape your left leg along the back of the couch. Find the normal force on your calf:

$$N_{calf} = m_{leg}g = 7kg \times 9.8\frac{m}{s^2} = 68.6N$$

You tuck your right arm under your right butt cheek, for a little extra angle on the hips and back. Determine the pressure on your butt as follows:

$$P_{butt} = \frac{F_{hand}}{A_{hand}} = \frac{m_{butt}g}{A_{hand}} = \frac{15kg \times 9.8\frac{m}{s^2}}{0.08m \times 0.15m} = 12kPa$$

You place your left arm over your eyes. Determine the angle of your elbow:

$$\varepsilon = 2\sin^{-1}\frac{\dfrac{w_{head}}{2}}{l_{contact}} = 2\sin^{-1}\frac{\dfrac{0.12m}{2}}{0.085m} = 89.8°$$

Your right leg is extended over the armrest. Find the pressure of the armrest on your leg:

$$P_{armrest} = \frac{F_{leg}}{A_{contact}} = \frac{m_{leg}g}{A_{contact}} = \frac{7kg \times 9.8\frac{m}{s^2}}{0.11m \times 0.21m} = 3kPa$$

With this type of expert precision in play, you, sir, will have the best nap of your life. No doubt.

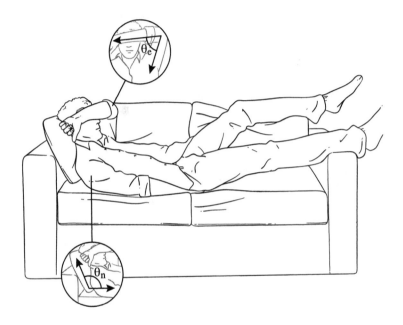

Fig. 6.a Find the Perfect Napping Position

6.b GET MORE COVERS

She's got the covers totally wrapped around her and is fast asleep. You need some more.

Determine the force you need to exert on the covers to get some. Assume she is a cylinder of

mass 59 kilograms and diameter 0.25 meter. You impart an angular acceleration of $\alpha = 0.017$

rad/s^2. Find the torque:

$$\tau = I\alpha = \frac{3mr^2}{2}\alpha = \frac{3 \times 59kg \times \left(\frac{0.25m}{2}\right)^2}{2} \cdot 0.017\frac{rad}{s^2} = 0.024Nm$$

Determine the force:

$$F = \frac{\tau}{r} = \frac{0.024Nm}{\frac{0.25m}{2}} = 0.19N$$

Find the length of covers you get in 7 seconds:

$$l = \frac{r\alpha t^2}{2} = \frac{0.25m \times 0.017\frac{rad}{s^2} \times (7s)^2}{2} = 0.10m$$

The important thing is not to wake her up as you unwind the covers from her. Easy does it.

F
d
α

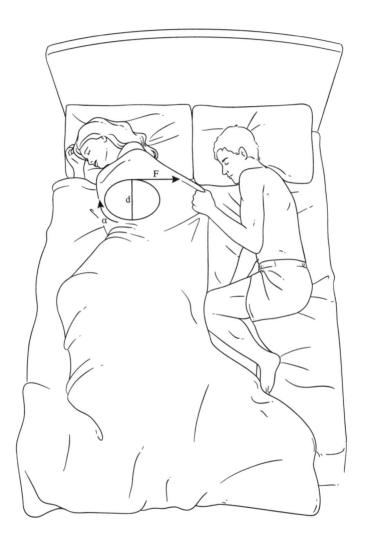

Fig. 6.b Get More Covers

6.c SCORE MORE SPACE IN BED

You determine to gain more bed space through the use of strategic spooning. Strategic spooning involves proactively taking the spooning position and then using advanced Man Physics tactics to move your bedmate to her side of the bed. Assume you are in the spooning position. The values involved are:

F_h: force used to move both your and her hips forward

F_r: force used to move everything else but your hips

m_{hh}: mass of her hips = 24 kilograms

m_{mh}: mass of your hips = 32 kilograms

m_{mr}: mass of everything else but your hips = 43 kilograms

μ: coefficient of friction between bed and hips = 0.6

d: distance of a hip move = 0.1 meter

Determine the energy you must exert with your hips to push her hips forward into a reverse spooning position:

$$\mathrm{E_{hips}} = \mathrm{F_h d} = (\mathrm{m_{hh}} + \mathrm{m_{mr}})\mathrm{g}\mu\mathrm{d} = (24\mathrm{kg} + 32\mathrm{kg})9.8\frac{\mathrm{m}}{\mathrm{s^s}} \times 0.6 \times 0.1\mathrm{m} = 33\mathrm{J}$$

The new position will not be as comfortable for you or her, so she will readjust by moving to a position that will facilitate comfortable spooning. After she readjusts, you take the normal spooning position again, thus moving toward her end of the bed. Calculate the energy required for you to readjust:

$$E_{rest} = F_r d = m_{mr} g \mu d = 43kg \times 9.8\frac{m}{s^s} \times 0.6 \times 0.1m = 25J$$

The total energy required in one move is then 58 joules. If you require more room, then repeat the process. To take advantage of your newly acquired real estate, see Escape a Spooning.

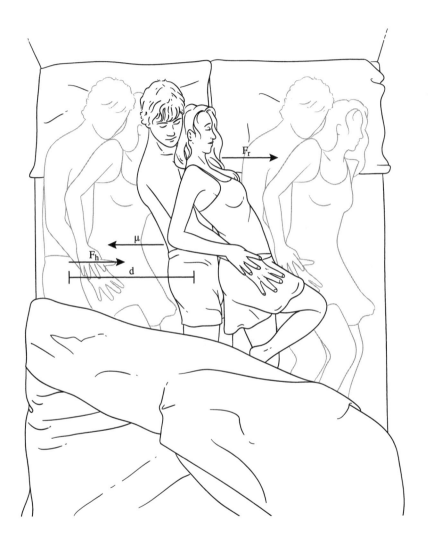

Fig. 6.c Score More Space in Bed

6.d SLEEP IN ON WEEKENDS

Sleeping in on the weekends is a God-given right. One of the things that gets in the way is the

alarm clock when you forget to turn off the alarm. For these instances (and only these

instances), you keep your girlfriend's teddy bear close to the bed. It becomes a lethal alarm

clock billy club, in your hands. Determine the momentum that you must give the teddy bear's

head to silence the clock. You know that the force it takes to push the alarm Off button is $F = 4.9$

newtons (N). The other components are:

m: mass of the head = 0.12 kilogram

Δt: time it takes the full-speed head to come to rest on the alarm clock = 0.43 second

Now you just need to apply Newton's Second Law:

$$F = \frac{m\Delta v}{\Delta t}$$

Solve for $m\Delta v$:

$$m\Delta v = F\Delta t = 4.9N \times 0.43 = 2.1Ns$$

The velocity that you must give to the head is:

$$v = \frac{2.1Ns}{m} = 17\frac{m}{s}$$

See—there is a reason you let her wuss up your bed with a stuffed animal.

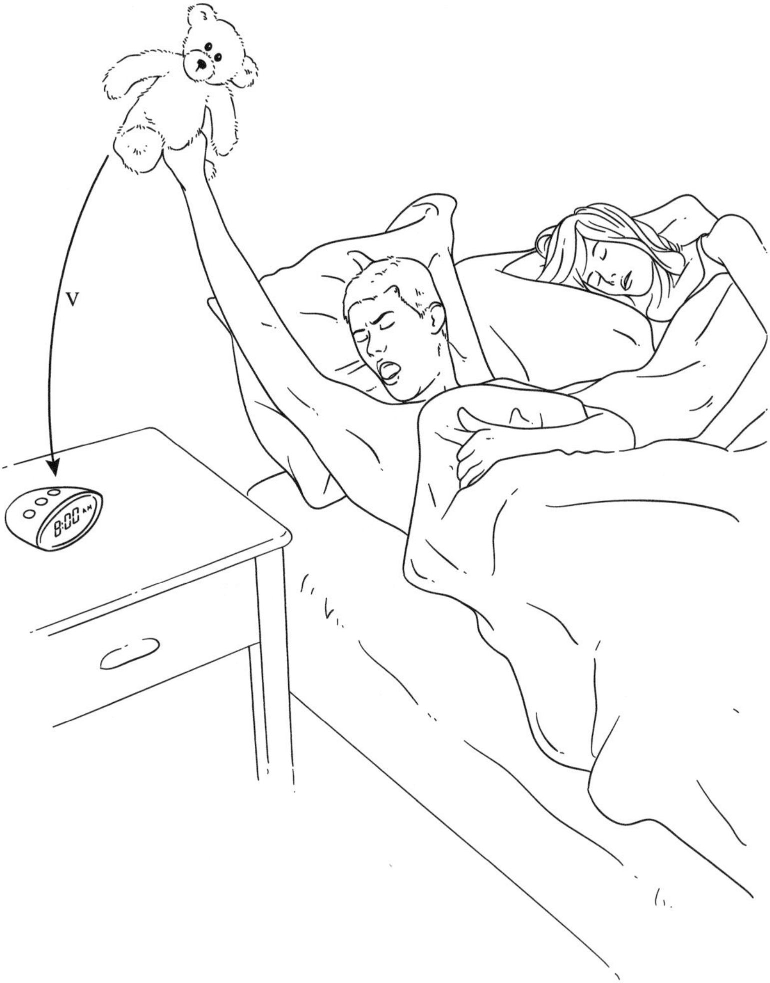
V
8:00 AM

Fig. 6.d Sleep In on Weekends

6.e SNORE AS MUCH AS YOU WANT

You are determined to sleep without getting the elbow. Utilize the sound-dampening

characteristics of pillows. Wait until she goes to sleep, and cover her head with the pillow.

Determine the thickness of pillow with which you must cover her ears. Assume the following:

$$E_p = E_s e^{-T/T_o}$$

Where:

E_s: sound energy of the snore at her ear

E_p: energy after dampening by pillow

T: thickness of pillow

T_o: thickness of pillow to give a reduction of $1/e$ in E_s = 5.53 meters

Calculate the thickness of pillow necessary to reduce E_s by 75%:

$$E_p = E_s e^{-T/T_o}$$
$$\frac{E_p}{E_s} = e^{-T/T_o} = 0.75$$
$$T = -T_o \ln 0.75 = -5.53m \times \ln 0.75 = 1.59m$$

To make a dent in the sound of your snore, you will need a pillow thickness of 1.59m. Determine

this thickness in feet:

$$T = 1.59m \times 3.28\frac{ft}{m} = 5.23 ft$$

So it looks like it's extra-thick pillows, or a nice set of earplugs—your call.

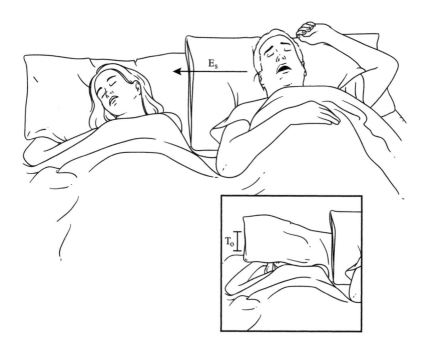

Fig. 6.e Snore as Much as You Want

6.f CRASH ON A COUCH

Inevitably, there will come a time (or many times) when you will need to crash on a buddy's couch. It may involve multiple nights and the possibility of getting tossed out when you have overstayed your welcome. You need to make sure you don't end up couchless. Of course, the harder it is to move you, the longer you can stay. Let's examine this tactic by using a hypothetical situation:

D: number of days stayed = 2

Y: number of years you have known your bud = 11

B: number of your buddy's beers you have downed during this stay = 23

T: number of times your buddy's wife has screamed upon discovering a lack of toilet paper in the bathroom since you have been there = 13

Find the probability that, under these circumstances, your buddy will try to physically remove you from the couch when you are sleeping:

$$P_{homeless} = \frac{D + B + T}{D + B + T + Y} \times 100 = \frac{2 + 23 + 13}{2 + 23 + 13 + 11} \times 100 = 77.6\%$$

Clearly, you must determine how to make it hardest to be lifted while sleeping. Utilize the couch crevices to your advantage. Calculate the effective increase in your mass when you brace a fist deep within the couch cushions. Here are the relevant variables:

F: force you had to use to bury your hand between the couch cushions and make a fist = 196 newtons

F_{lift} = force your buddy must exert to lift you

m: your mass = 71 kilograms

$$F_{lift} = mg + F = 71kg \times 9.8\frac{m}{s^2} + 196N = 892N$$

Determine the equivalent mass that your buddy would have to be able to lift:

$$m_{equ} = \frac{892N}{9.8\frac{m}{s^2}} = 91kg$$

While you might not have a place to call your own, you sure can hold your own. Your couch-crashing skills will be far superior to the average freeloader when you add some physics to the equation.

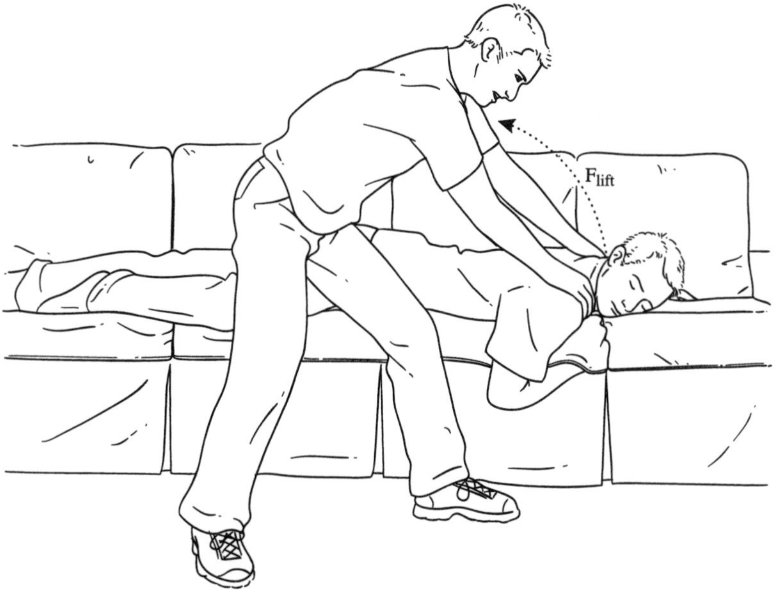
Flift

Fig. 6.f Crash on a Couch

6.g SLEEP ON A HAMMOCK WITHOUT FLIPPING

You know there is no better way to enjoy a summer day than to take an afternoon nap in the hammock, gently swinging in the breeze. You determine the period of the swing as follows:

l: distance of the center of mass about the axis of rotation = 0.76 meter:

$$T = \sqrt{\frac{l}{g}} = \sqrt{\frac{0.76m}{9.8\frac{m}{s^2}}} = 0.3s$$

Determine the maximum starting swing angle that you can adopt without tipping out of the hammock. You will need these additional values:

τ: torque necessary to tip hammock = 30 newton•meters

m: your mass = 70 kilograms

r: distance of center of mass from axis about which hammock tips = 0.1 meter

ϑ: start angle

Thus:

$$\tau = rmg\sin\theta$$
$$\theta = \sin^{-1}\frac{\tau}{rmg} = \sin^{-1}\frac{30N}{0.1m \times 70kg \times 9.8\frac{m}{s^2}} = 26°$$

Now determine how far you can move your center of mass from the center of the hammock when you roll over in your sleep:

$$r_{roll} = \frac{\tau}{mg} = \frac{30Nm}{70kg \times 9.8\frac{m}{s^2}} = 0.04m$$

Feel that breeze!

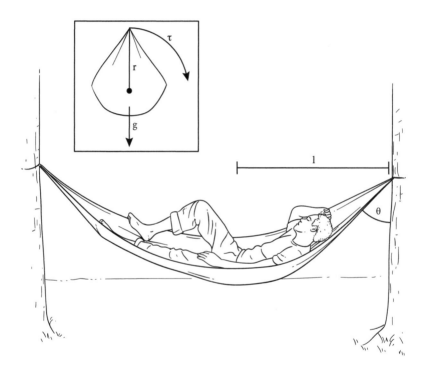

Fig. 6.g Sleep on a Hammock Without Flipping

LESSONS IN THIS CHAPTER

FEATS OF GREATNESS

7.a AVOID A VISIT WITH THE MOTHER-IN-LAW

Sorry to break this to you, but at some point you may end up with a mother-in-law that isn't the most pleasant person. You may have to have dinner with her. Unless, unless, . . . unless a broken bone prevents it. You determine the speed with which your pinkie must hit the ground from a "fall" in order to break it as an excuse for not being able to go to dinner.

E_{break}: energy necessary to break pinkie = 490 joules (J)

$$v = \sqrt{\frac{2E_{break}}{m}} = \sqrt{\frac{2 \times 490J}{80kg}} = 3.5\frac{m}{s}$$

The height of your center of mass required for your pinkie to reach this speed is:

$$h = \frac{E_{break}}{mg} = \frac{490J}{80kg \times 9.8\frac{m}{s^2}} = 0.63m$$

A fall from 63 centimeters with the full energy of the fall on your pinkie, should do it. You could always say you accidentally rolled out of bed, tipped over on the barstool, or fell while dusting the top of the bookshelf—though she probably won't buy that last one.

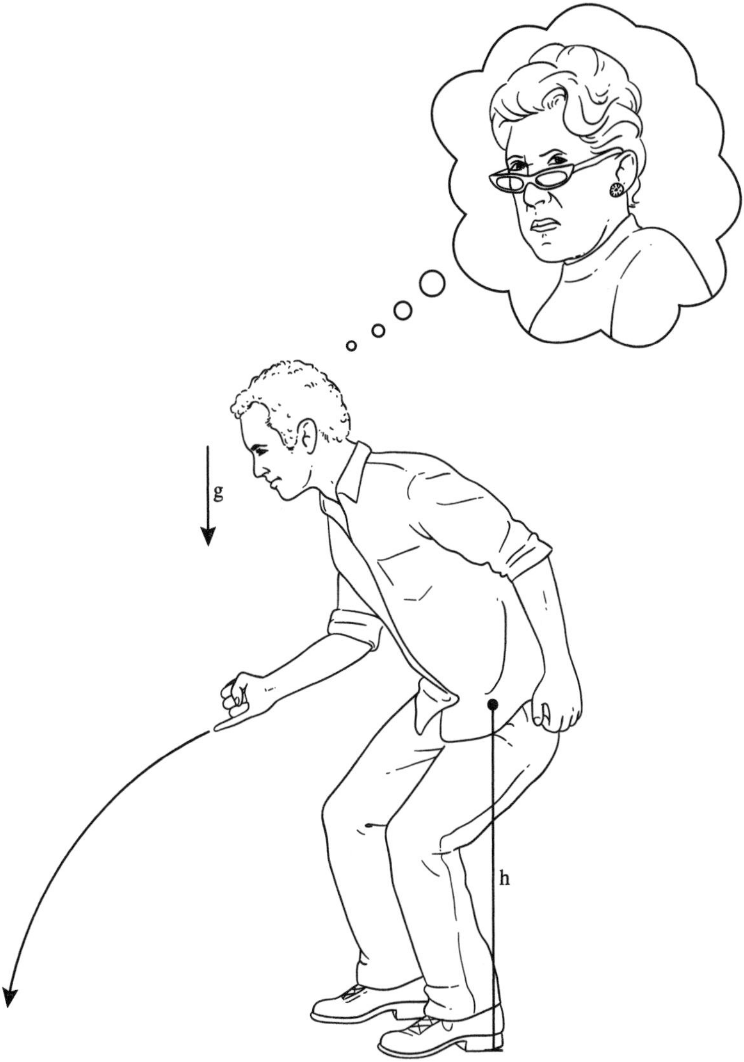
g
h

Fig. 7.a Avoid a Visit with the Mother-in-Law

7.b GET TO WORK ON TIME

Too much time spent on escaping the spoon last night. This is what you get: You're going to be late for work again. Now you must determine the fastest way to get there. You have two options: (1) the shorter route with traffic and (2) the much longer route with no traffic. Calculate the times for both routes on the basis of the following known variables.

Route 1

d_1: distance = 7 miles

s_1: average speed, allowing for rush-hour traffic = 21 miles/hour

n_1: number of traffic lights = 6

t_{lights}: average time spent at traffic lights = 63 seconds

$$t_1 = \frac{d_1}{s_1} + n_1 t_{lights} = \frac{7mi}{21\frac{mi}{hr}} + 6 \times \frac{63s}{3600\frac{s}{hr}} = 0.438hr$$

Route 2

d_{21}: distance traveled with speed of 60 mi/hr = 10 mi

d_{22}: distance traveled with speed of 20 mi/hr = 0.4 mi

d_{23}: distance traveled with a speed of 37 mi/hr = 5.3 mi

n_2: number of traffic lights = 3

$$t_2 = \frac{d_{21}}{60\frac{mi}{hr}} + \frac{d_{22}}{20\frac{mi}{hr}} + \frac{d_{23}}{37\frac{mi}{hr}} + n_1 t_{lights} = \frac{10}{60\frac{mi}{hr}} + \frac{0.4}{20\frac{mi}{hr}} + \frac{5.3mi}{37\frac{mi}{hr}} + 3 \times \frac{63s}{3600\frac{s}{hr}} = 0.382hr$$

You determine that even though the second option is longer and involves traveling in a school zone, it is the quickest way for you to get to work.

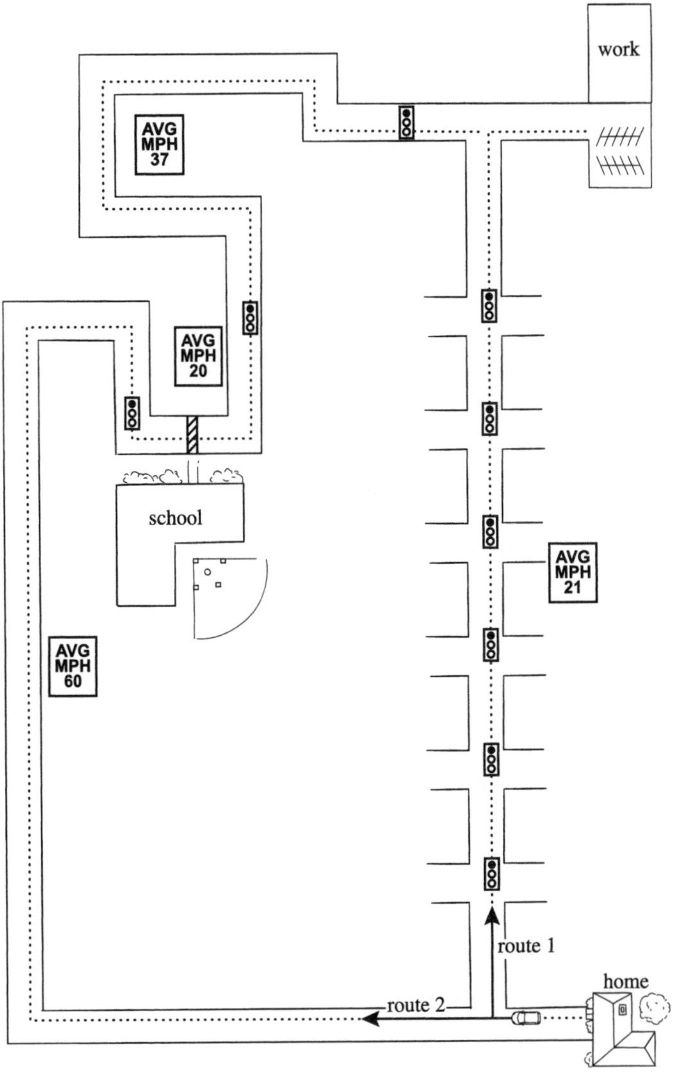
work
AVG MPH 37
AVG MPH 20
school
AVG MPH 21
AVG MPH 60
route 1
home
route 2

Fig. 7.b Get to Work on Time

7.c BYPASS STADIUM TRAFFIC

If you aren't going to the game, the traffic is absolutely unwelcome. You determine the best way around it, not only because you can, but also because you want to impress your girlfriend in the passenger seat. You calculate the time it would take to skirt the traffic in either a clockwise or a counterclockwise fashion. For the counterclockwise direction:

n: number of traffic lights = 13

t_{lights}: average time spent at traffic lights = 63 seconds

t_{left}: average time spent making left turns at intersections = 26 seconds

d: distance to travel = 3 miles

s: average traveling speed = 35 miles/hour

$$t_{ccw} = \frac{d}{s} + nt_{lights} + nt_{left} = \frac{3mi}{35\frac{mi}{hr}} + 13 \times \frac{63s}{3600\frac{s}{hr}} + 13 \times \frac{26s}{3600\frac{s}{hr}} = 0.407hr$$

In the clockwise direction:

n: number of traffic lights = 13

t_{right}: average time spent at traffic lights before making a right on red = 23 seconds

d: distance to travel = 3 miles

s: average traveling speed = 35 miles/hour

$$t_{cw} = \frac{d}{s} + nt_{right} = \frac{3mi}{35\frac{mi}{hr}} + 13 \times \frac{23s}{3600\frac{s}{hr}} = 0.169hr$$

You take the clockwise direction to skirt the traffic, saving tons of time and traffic aggravation.

Your girlfriend is quite impressed too. She'll probably jump your bones tonight.

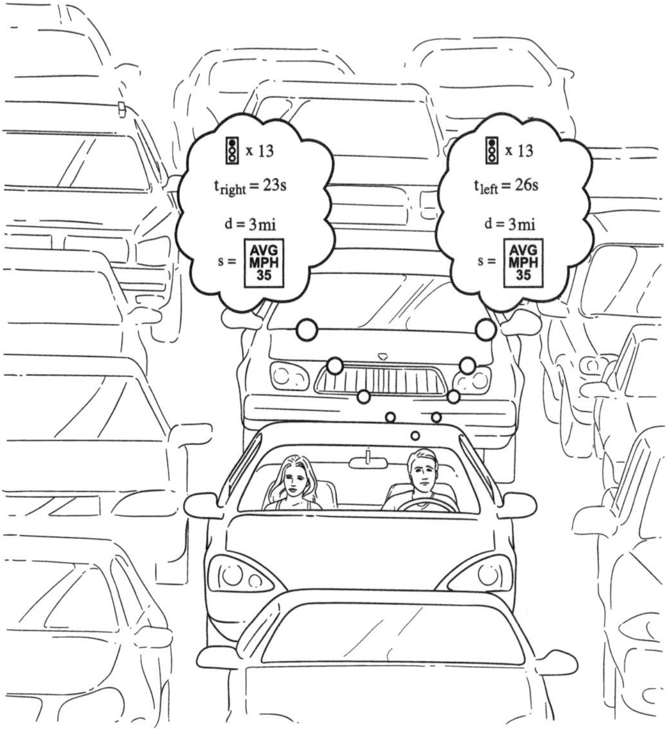
x 13
$t_{right} = 23s$
d = 3mi
s = AVG MPH 35
x 13
$t_{left} = 26s$
d = 3mi
s = AVG MPH 35

Fig. 7.c Bypass Stadium Traffic

7.d FIT INTO A TIGHT PARKING SPOT

You use the theory of special relativity to determine the necessary speed to parallel-park in a space too short for your ride.

l_{space}: length of space = 4.1 meters

l_{car}: length of your car = 4.24 meters

$$l_{space} = \frac{l_{car}}{\gamma} = \sqrt{1 - \frac{v^2}{c^2}} \, l_{car}$$

Solve for v in terms of c:

$$v = c\sqrt{1 - \left(\frac{l_{space}}{l_{car}}\right)^2} = c\sqrt{1 - \left(\frac{4.1m}{4.24}\right)^2} = 0.25c$$

So in order to pull this off, you pretty much need to be traveling at about a ¼ the speed of light.

Not a big deal, right? While you're at it, why don't you just call up Doc and ask if you can borrow the DeLorean?

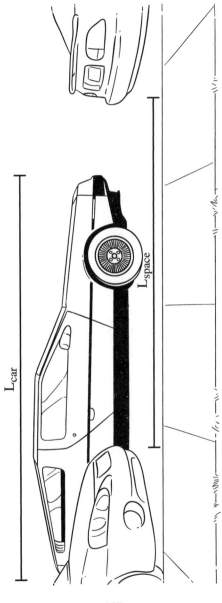

Fig. 7.d Fit Into a Tight Parking Spot

7.e IRON A SHIRT SO IT LOOKS LIKE IT WAS DRYCLEANED

It is all about wrinkles and creases. You find the most efficient way to remove the wrinkles and add the creases. The relevant values follow:

t: time it takes iron to remove wrinkles, in 1 placement, without burning shirt = 6 seconds

A_{iron}: area of iron = 0.012 square meter (m^2)

A_{shirt}: area of shirt = 0.5 m^2

m: mass of iron = 1.3 kilogram

μ: coefficient of kinetic friction between iron and shirt = 0.28

Determine the minimum number of iron placements necessary:

$$N = \frac{A_{shirt}}{A_{iron}} = \frac{0.5m^2}{0.012m^2} = 42$$

Find the time it takes to complete *N* placements:

$$t_{iron} = Nt = 42 \times 6s = 252s$$

Now determine whether it takes less energy to lift the iron 1 millimeter and move it between placements or to push it a distance of 0.08 meter:

$$\mathrm{E_{lift} = Nmgh = 42 \times 1.3kg \times 9.8\frac{m}{s^2} \times 0.001m = 0.54J}$$

$$\mathrm{E_{push}} = (\mathrm{N} - 1)\mathrm{mg}\mu\mathrm{d} = (42 - 1) \times 1.3\mathrm{kg} \times 9.8\frac{\mathrm{m}}{\mathrm{s}^2} \times 0.28 \times 0.08\mathrm{m} = 12\mathrm{J}$$

You determine that lifting the iron between placements is the best way to achieve the properly pressed shirt.

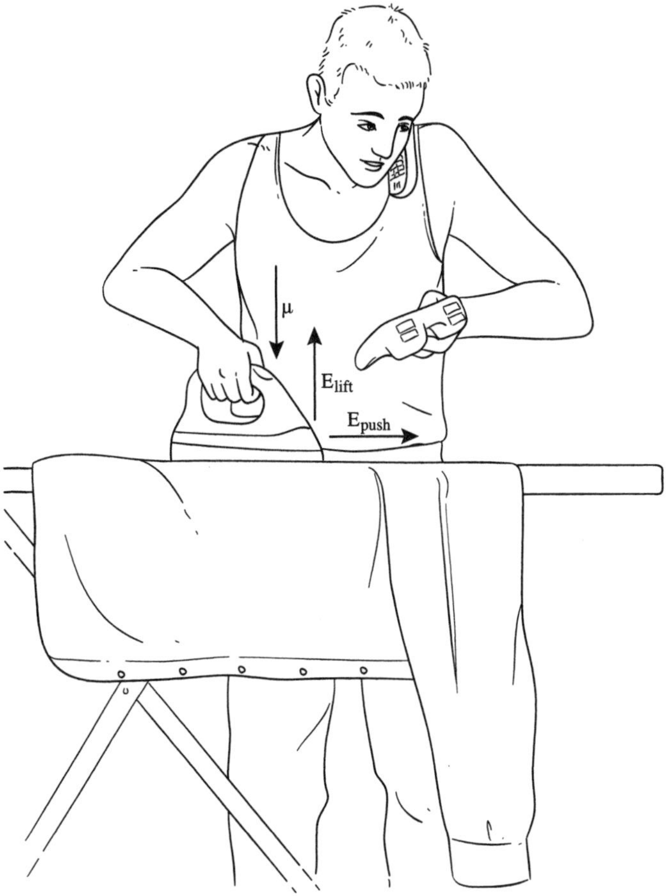
μ
Elift
Epush

Fig. 7.e Iron a Shirt So It Looks Like It Was Drycleaned

7.f TIE A WINDSOR KNOT

A night out on the town at the show calls for a Windsor knot. Problem is you are running late

from your afternoon nap (see Find the Perfect Napping Position) and your wife is putting

pressure on you. Calculate the effect of this pressure on the time it will take you to tie your tie:

$$t = \frac{(V-S)t_{harass}}{t_{nap}} t_0$$

Where:

V: how loudly she is telling you to hurry (scale of 1 to 10) = 7

S: ratio of length of her leg to length of her skirt = 2

t_{nap}: how long you napped = 420 minutes

t_{harass}: how long she has been harassing you to get ready = 422 minutes

t_0: normal time it takes you to tie your tie = 32 seconds

Thus:

$$t = \frac{(V-S)t_{harass}}{t_{nap}} t_0 = \frac{(7-2)422\,min}{420\,min} \times 32s = 161s$$

Now determine the force with which you must hold the knot of the tie in place while tying. For

this, you need:

μ: coefficient of friction between tie material and fingers = 0.5

f: force with which you are pulling on tie = 4 newtons (N)

N: normal force of hold

$$N = \frac{f}{\mu} = \frac{4N}{0.5} = 8N$$

Of course your knot comes out perfectly, and as a result, she throws you onto the bed and has

her way with you, show be damned.

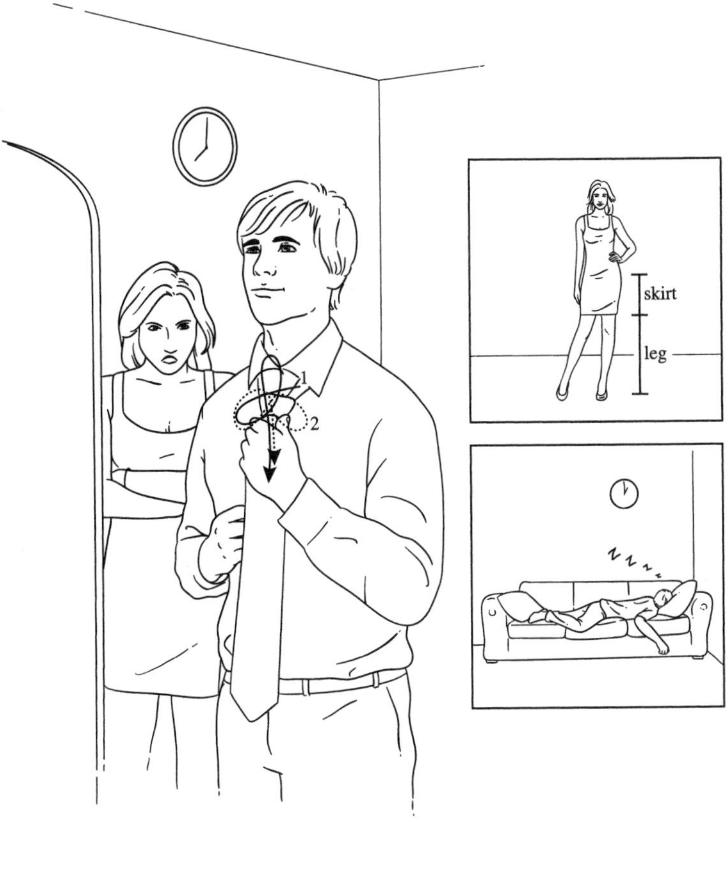
1
2
skirt
leg

Fig. 7.f Tie a Windsor Knot

7.g FIGHT OFF A BEAR

Out in the wild, you are left to your own devices. On this trip you are out in the wild, and a bear

is wanting some of what you have, but all you have are your fists. You determine the correct

timing to land a knockout punch squarely on the bear's nose.

s_{bear}: speed at which bear is charging toward you = 30 miles/hour

l_{arm}: length of your arm = 1.1 meter

a_{avg}: average acceleration of your fist = 76 m/s^2

Find the time it takes you to throw the punch:

$$t = \sqrt{\frac{2l_{arm}}{a_{avg}}} = \sqrt{\frac{2 \times 1.1m}{76\frac{m}{s^2}}} = 0.17s$$

Determine how far the bear travels in this time:

$$d = s_{bear}t = 30\frac{mi}{hr} \times \frac{1hr}{3600s} \times \frac{1609m}{1mi} \times 0.17s = 0.39m$$

You discover that the bear must be 0.39 + 1.1 = 1.49 meters away from you, at full charge, when

you let loose with your knockout blow.

S_{bear}
d
L_{arm}

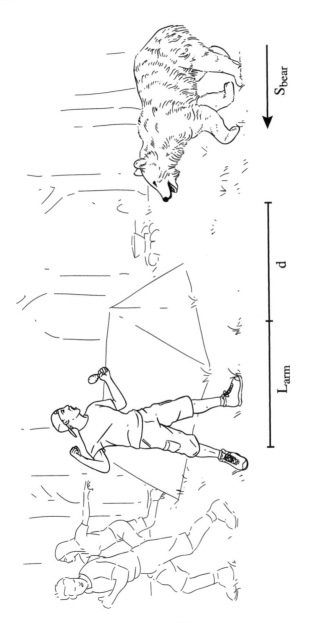

Fig. 7.g Fight Off a Bear

7.h LIGHT A CAMPFIRE IN THE WIND

Too windy to be able to light a campfire? Nonsense! You use a three-quarters hand ax, some

mud, several stones, and grass thatching to build a little wind block. Calculate the momentum

you generate for the ax blade while chopping:

$$p_{ax} = m_{ax}s_{ax} = 2kg \times 12\frac{m}{s} = 24\frac{kg \bullet m}{s}$$

Where:

m_{ax}: mass of the head of the ax = 2 kilograms

s: speed of the head at impact = 12 meters/second

Determine the momentum of a tree falling in the woods:

$$p_{tree} = m_{tree}s_{tree} = m\sqrt{2gh} = 583kg \times \sqrt{2 \times 9.8\frac{m}{s^2} \times 10m} = 8,200\frac{kg \bullet m}{s}$$

Where:

h: height of the center of mass of the tree = 10 meters

m_{tree}: mass of tree = 583 kilograms

Form logs of length 4 meters, and notch the ends of the logs to fit together. Stack stones about

the fire pit. Use the mud to shore up both the stones and the stacked logs. Repeat the process

about all sides of the fire pit, tapering the stack of stones as the stack gets higher. When the

height is to your liking, use the grass thatching to cover the wooden part of the structure. Now

you have built a wind block for your campfire.

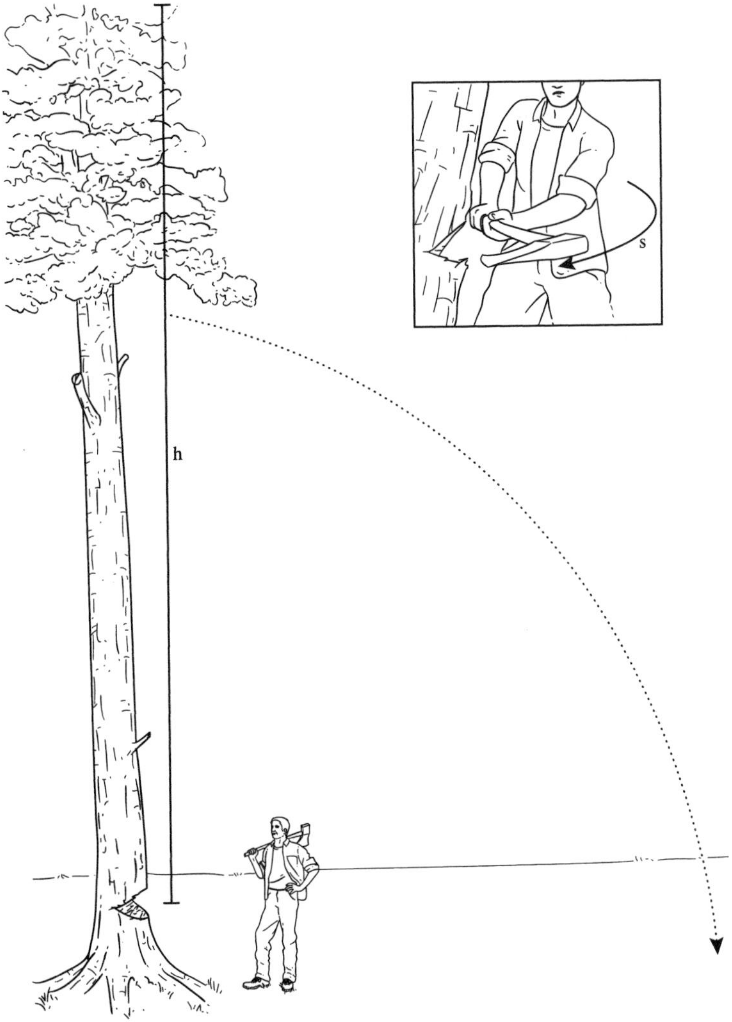
s
h

Fig. 7.h Light a Campfire in the Wind

7.i PUT OUT A FIRE

You are ready to leave a campsite, and the last thing to do is put out the campfire. Determine

which is the less taxing way to do it: shovel dirt onto it or douse it with water?

N_{shovel}: number of shovels full of dirt = 7

$N_{buckets}$: number of buckets of water = 3

m_{shovel}: mass of dirt and shovel = 1.8 kilograms

m_{bucket}: mass of water and bucket = 4 kilograms

d: distance to water spigot = 30 meters

h: height to which shovel and bucket must be lifted = 1 meter

Calculate the energy expenditure required in each case:

$$E_{shovel} = N_{shovel}mgh = 7 \times 1.8kg \times 9.8\frac{m}{s^2} \times 1m = 123J$$

$$E_{buckets} = N_{buckets}m_{bucket}gh = 3 \times 5kg \times 9.8\frac{m}{s^2} \times 1m = 147J$$

You determine that it is easier to shovel the dirt; in fact, it's as easy as 1-2-3!

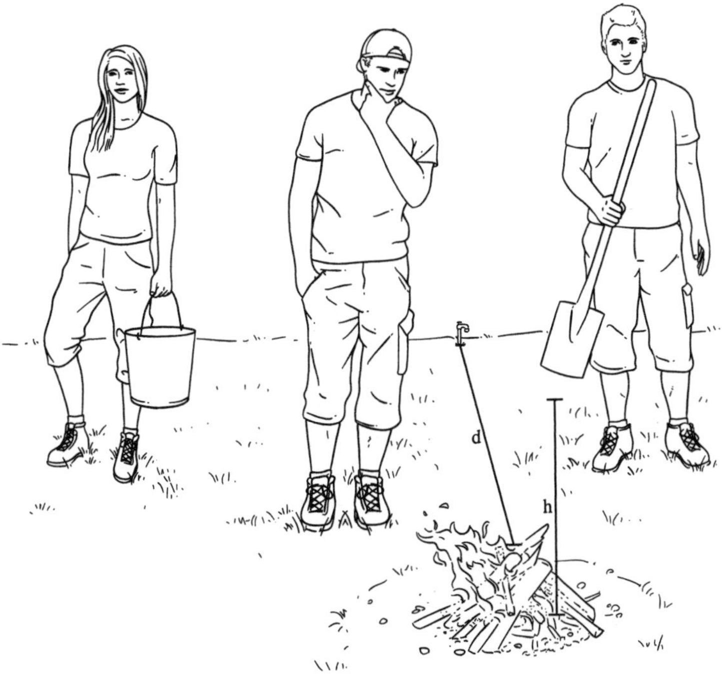
d
h

Fig. 7i Put Out a Fire

7.j BREAK UP A BAR FIGHT

You turn your back for a second and all hell breaks loose! Your buddy is face-to-face with some

guy, and you can see it's moving in the direction of fisticuffs. Determine the time you have to

intervene in an effort to avoid bloodshed. First you must make some rapid calculations:

t_{fist}: time it takes your buddy to make a fist = 0.2 second

t_{load}: time it takes your buddy to load up his punch = 0.4 second

a_{fist}: acceleration of your buddy's fist = 60 m/s^2

a_{carry}: acceleration with which you can carry your buddy away from the fight = 4 m/s^2

l: length of your buddy's reach = 0.97 meter

Now determine the distance from danger that you can move your buddy in the time it takes him

to throw a punch:

$$d_{prepunch} = \frac{a_{carry}\left(t_{fist} + t_{load}\right)^2}{2} = \frac{4\frac{m}{s^2}\left(0.2s + 0.4s\right)^2}{2} = 0.72m$$

and the speed with which you are moving your bud back when he launches:

$$s_{retreat} = a_{carry}\left(t_{fist} + t_{load}\right) = 4\frac{m}{s^2}\left(0.2s + 0.4s\right) = 2.4\frac{m}{s}$$

Then find the time it takes your bud's fist to overcome this velocity:

$$t_{throw} = \frac{s_{retreat}}{a_{fist} - a_{carry}} = \frac{2.4\frac{m}{s}}{60\frac{m}{s^2} - 4\frac{m}{s^2}} = 0.04s$$

You realize that you must intercept your buddy with additional time to ensure that he doesn't

land his sucker punch. Find how much more time you need so that he is out of range when he

punches by applying this formula:

$$t = \sqrt{\frac{2l}{a_{carry}}} = \sqrt{\frac{2 \times 0.97m}{4\frac{m}{s^2}}} = 0.7s$$

To save a couple of dudes from blackened eyes, you must start the intervention 0.1 second before your friend even makes a fist. Get going!

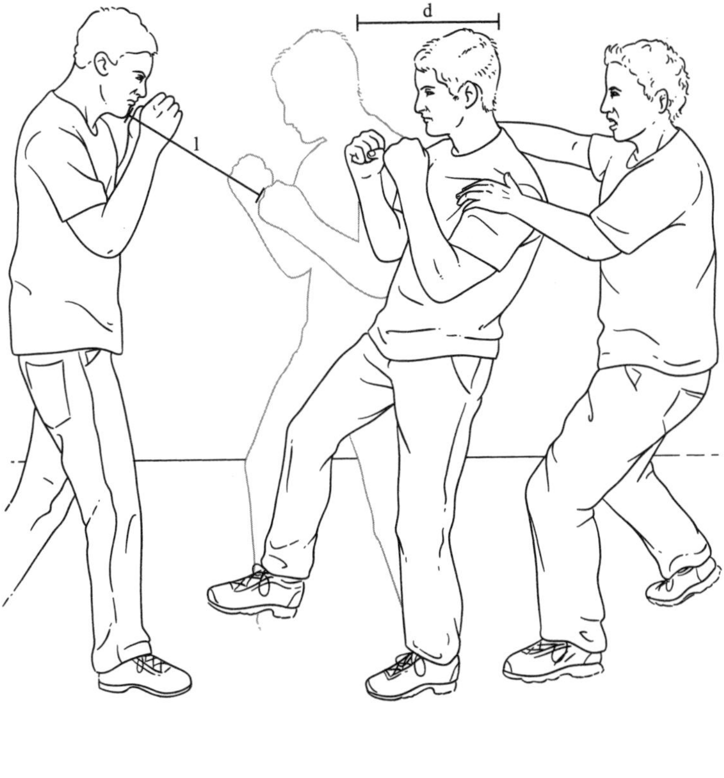
d
l

Fig. 7.j Break Up a Bar Fight

7.k CLIFF DIVE

Extreme diving. You determine what initial rotational speed you need to generate the back triple with four twists. The height of the dive is 26 meters. Calculate the time you have to complete the rotations:

$$t = \sqrt{\frac{2h}{g}} = \sqrt{\frac{2 \times 26m}{9.8\frac{m}{s^2}}} = 5.3s$$

Calculate the rotational speed for the triple:

$$\omega_3 = \frac{\theta}{t} = \frac{3 \times 2\pi}{5.3s} = 3.6\frac{rad}{s}$$

Calculate the rotational speed for the four twists:

$$\omega_4 = \frac{\theta}{t} = \frac{4 \times 2\pi}{5.3s} = 4.7\frac{rad}{s}$$

Since this is the most difficult dive ever done in competition, you take the gold.

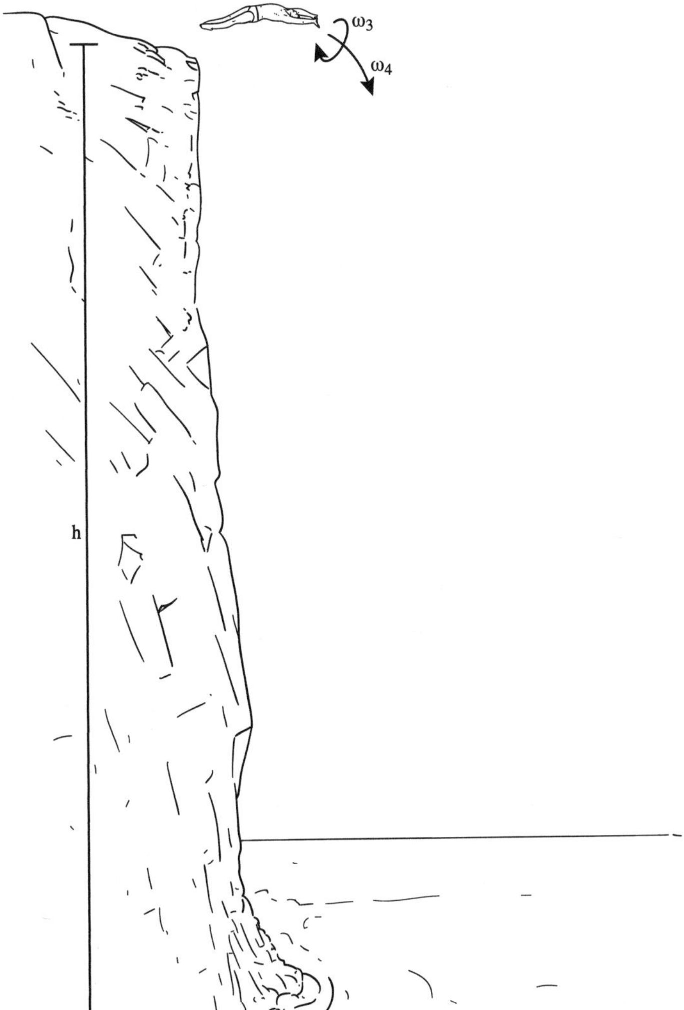
ω3
ω4
h

Fig. 7.k Cliff Dive

7.I DO A DOUGHNUT

Show off those wheels. Lay down the rubber; do a doughnut. Determine the minimum forward

speed you need to get the doughnut going. Apply Newton's Second Law:

m: mass of the car = 1,636 kilograms

μ: coefficient of kinetic friction between tires and asphalt = 0.6

s: forward speed

r: radius of the turn = 5 meters

F_c: centripetal force

f_k: force of kinetic friction between tires and asphalt

g: gravity

$$F_c = f_k$$
$$\frac{s^2}{r}m = mg\mu$$
$$s = \sqrt{rg\mu} = \sqrt{5m \times 9.8\frac{m}{s^2} \times 0.6} = 5.4\frac{m}{s}$$

Make sure once you've sufficiently impressed the teenagers hanging out, you top off your

doughnut by burning out of the parking lot. And while Newton's Second Law helped to pull

off the doughnut, it won't help when you get pulled over by the actual law.

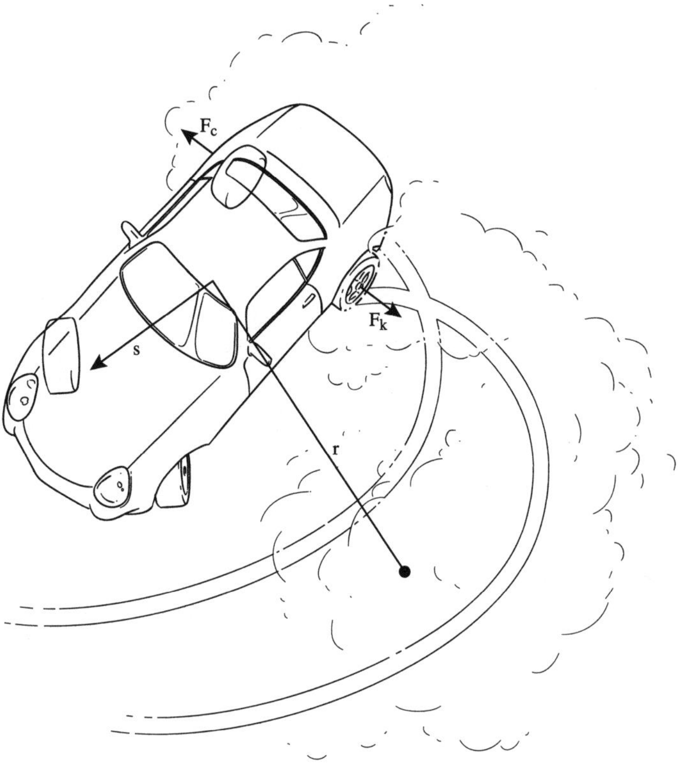
F_c
F_k
s
r

Fig. 7.1 Do a Doughnut

INDEX